*Remember Pearl Harbor!*

## *Also by* BLAKE CLARK:

PARADISE LIMITED
*An Informal History of the Fabulous Hawaiians*

OMAI: First Polynesian Ambassador to England

ORIENTAL ENGLAND

# Remember Pearl Harbor!

BLAKE CLARK

MODERN AGE BOOKS · NEW YORK

PUBLISHED BY MODERN AGE BOOKS



FIRST PRINTING, FEBRUARY, 1942
SECOND PRINTING, MAY, 1942
THIRD PRINTING, JULY, 1942
FOURTH PRINTING, AUGUST, 1942

BMG • UOPWA 18

PRINTED IN THE UNITED STATES OF AMERICA

*By Ruttle, Shaw & Wetherill, Philadelphia, Pa.*

TO THE HEROIC DEFENDERS
OF WAKE

# *Acknowledgments*

MY GREATEST AID in telling the story of Pearl Harbor naturally came from the scores of officers, chaplains, nurses, and fighting men whose individual stories combine into the single narrative. Many of these persons are named in the book. Many are not, for reasons of their own. I thank them all.

# Contents

*Remember Pearl Harbor!*

# *This Is Honolulu*

ALL MY LIFE I have wanted to live history. I would feel cheated indeed if I had lived through the age of Napoleon and not seen at first hand the Paris mob, the march to Moscow, or the Battle of Waterloo. Ever since I read the book, I have envied John Reed and Boardman Robinson the ten days that shook the world. I would like to have been in Europe during the First World War. I do not crave sensation merely, nor dream of a life of adventure. I never envied Richard Halliburton's individualistic exploits. What I have wanted is to be present when significant history is in the making.

I have had my wish. I have been very close to some of the horrors and glories of one of the most crucial battles in America's history. I did not see it all with my own eyes. I was not everywhere at once, as all men would have liked to be—at Hickam Field manning an anti-aircraft gun, in a pursuit plane fighting off Japanese bombers over Pearl Harbor, in a motor car racing out to Tripler Hospital with blood plasma. But from what I did see with my own eyes and from talking to friends and others who were in all the different centers of action "when it happened," I have lived through real history—the history of Pearl Harbor. Its beginning is as calm as the South Seas, and its ending is as angry and determined as the U.S. Marines who cry for revenge of Wake Island.

Honolulu is one of the calmest, sunniest, most delightfully peaceful cities in the world. Its name means "Fair Haven," and a fair haven it has been to millions of people in the course of its history. Sundays are especially quiet here. It is like a small New England town. Cars hardly start moving before ten o'clock. We have late breakfasts; then the young are off to the beach, the old to church. On that particular Sunday it seemed more peaceful than usual. The broad Pacific washed upon the shores of Oahu so gently that the Waikiki waves were too small to attract early Sunday surfers. There were so few clouds that the top of Mount Tantalus behind the city showed more than clear against the sky.

Most of us were just getting out of bed or having breakfast when the shooting started. I heard the rumbling noise of coast artillery practice, as I thought, and came on down to read the Sunday *Advertiser* before breakfast. Our copy had not come. It was the first time I had ever known it not to be there. When I walked down to Blackshear's drug store around the corner, the druggist smiled as I picked up the last copy and said,

"Nobody got their paper this morning. Heard the presses broke down. This is an early edition."

Mr. and Mrs. Frear, with whom I am living on Punahou Street, were already seated when I came back. I gave Mr. Frear the paper and he read "the juicy bits" to us as we ate our waffles and bacon. Divorces were very numerous in Honolulu now, he read. "All a woman has to do to get a divorce these days is say her husband doesn't keep his shirt clean," he observed, smiling at himself for the reactionary remark. Looking back at the paper, he read that we should send safety razor blades to the British soldiers, because steel was short now, and nothing helped a Tommy's morale like a clean shave. The rumbling outside continued.

Yamato came running in. "Plenty plane outside!" he exclaimed. "Come see!"

Led by the little Japanese, we went to the back porch. We could see a squadron of planes high above. Over Pearl Harbor we saw the sky dotted with black puffs of anti-aircraft smoke, hanging heavily in the air.

"That's good," said Mr. Frear. "We *ought* to get ready."

Miss Claire, our neighbor, who has retired from Punahou School where she taught the town's grandparents, parents, and children, came running through the house.

"We're under attack! The Japanese are bombing

Oahu!" she said, looking apologetically at Yamato and his fat little wife Hatsu.

"Oh, no, it's only practice. Don't get excited, Claire," said Mr. Frear, and we all chimed in reassuringly. Poor Miss Claire retired, convinced she had been the victim of rumor.

In a few minutes she had her revenge, though not one which she relished. As we were finishing our breakfast, we saw her again running across the lawn.

"If you don't believe it, turn on your radio!" she exclaimed as she came in.

I checked the dial. "Keep calm, everybody. Oahu is under attack. This is no joke. It's the real McCoy. The emblem of the Rising Sun has been seen on the wings of the attacking planes." I recognized the dynamic voice of Webley Edwards, KGMB station manager.

The first thing I thought was "Hatsu and Yamato—what will they do?"

Yamato and Hatsu both are alien Japanese. Neither speaks English well. They subscribe to the Japanese paper here, and they have a good short-wave radio on which they pick up news broadcasts from Japan every night after they retire to the servants' quarters at the rear of the lawn. Their seventeen-year-old son, Shigeru, has just returned from Japan, where they sent him to be educated. Yamato is a very efficient little fellow. I would choose him to execute almost any kind of plan. I have insisted that the loyalty of the Japanese in

Hawaii, the great majority at least, is unquestionable, but I confess that at the moment I became convinced of the attack, I had more hope than conviction that I had been right.

We called them from the kitchen and told them what the radio had announced.

Yamato smiled. "I don't think so," he said uncertainly.

Hatsu said, "No. They no fight. In Washington, Kurusu—you know Kurusu and Plesident still talk. No fight yet. Still talk."

As we gradually convinced them, Hatsu became physically ill. She and Mrs. Frear both cried, and they hugged each other, weeping, assuring each other that they understood, that no matter what happened they had been friends for years and would continue to be so in the years to come.

A light blue car turned into the driveway, bumped across the sidewalk, and came to a quick stop under the portico. A buxom little woman in Red Cross uniform ran up the steps. It was Mrs. C——, wife of the commander of one of the ships here. We had not recognized her at first in her Red Cross cap and gray dress.

"I'm bringing some girls from the ship here to spend the night," she announced. "They need to be near the maternity hospital down the street in case of emergency."

"What are you doing?" she said, turning to me.

"Come on. I need a man to help me evacuate people."

I climbed in, and Mrs. C— shot out of the driveway.

I was on my way to my first taste of history in the making.

"We're going first to Mabel's," she said. "I'm checking with every woman connected with our ship and being sure they are taken care of, out of the danger zones, near the hospital if they are about to have babies."

"What's happened? How much damage is done? How many planes attacked? What's going on?" I asked.

"The Japs slipped in," she said. "Went right into Pearl Harbor."

And she went on to tell the damage that had been done—the flying fields attacked, the ships disabled, the smoke rising from Pearl Harbor, the oil burning on top of the water, men swimming in it, the hundreds of wounded being rushed to the hospitals, the death of Admiral Kidd. "More damage in one hour than the U.S. fleet suffered in the entire World War! . . .

"They say two small subs got in the Harbor. I don't believe it. I don't believe they could get through. We don't know how it happened, but it's awful!"

We arrived at Mabel's on Pacific Heights. She had everything packed that she would need for several days. I carted it down, helped her and her little boy into the car. She told us about the bomb that struck the house a few doors below. It had torn away one whole end of the place, but had not harmed the dining room where the whole family were having breakfast. She and Mrs. C— wondered whether "their ship" was in the harbor and whether it was one of those bombed. Mrs. C—'s son-in-law, Bill, is a gunnery officer on the same ship.

"If Bill doesn't get one of those Jap carriers, I'll not let him in the house," she said.

All day long we drove through the streets.

Every few minutes we saw reminders of the attack. Driving along Kuhio Street at Waikiki, we came upon a house wrecked by a bomb which had exploded in the lawn. Even more sorrowful a spectacle than the house, I thought, was a coconut tree with its plumes blown off, leaving its strong, ugly stump staring at the sky. Across the canal, where McCully meets King Street, half a block of smoking, charred ruins were all that was left of the drug store where I used to buy my safety razor blades. It was completely wiped out, and, with it, the owner, his wife, and two girls who lived upstairs above the store.

In the lawn of Washington Place, the home of Governor Poindexter, a crowd of men stood looking into a wide hole left by a bomb. A photographer was taking a picture of a man standing shoulder deep in the bomb-pit, holding up a piece of shrapnel.

A dead Chinese man lay on the sidewalk near the shattered windows of the Schumann Carriage Company.

At the lower edge of Alewa Heights, we drove around a gaping hole in the asphalt pavement. Children were running up the street to where a part-Hawaiian man was holding a limp young girl in his arms. The family of five had been standing on the doorstep when the bomb fell. A piece of shrapnel had flown straight to the girl's heart. The man looked helplessly about him for a moment, then ran up the steps of his home and disappeared into the house with his dead daughter.

On Judd Street, near Iolani School, a five-passenger automobile lay in a twisted wreck. Fragments of fenders and glass had been blown across the road. A direct hit from above had killed the four men who were riding in it.

Bit by bit, we began to see what had happened. The Japanese, while their ambassador in Washington "still talk," had slipped up on the unsuspecting island under cover of darkness. Undoubtedly itching to drop their bombs on Pearl Harbor, their chief objective, and get away, they had first attacked each airport, bombing the hangars and mercilessly strafing the unprotected planes, lined up in orderly rows on the clean fields. Then, feeling relatively secure from pursuit and retaliation, they flew to Pearl Harbor and bombed the ships lying at anchor there.

We were quiet as we listened to each new story. We felt sick at our stomachs. Letting the damn Japs slip in and throw our own scrap-iron back in our faces! Fortunately, we were too busy to feel helpless. Mrs. C—— and, through her, the American Red Cross, had us in tow. They knew there were things to be done and they knew how to do them.

I began to feel better. I had a job to do, even though it was a small one—a grown-up man, following a woman around. In Kahala we passed Montgomery Clark and another fellow going from house to house, already on the job as fire wardens. "Have your garden hose ready for regular fire. Get a bucket of sand to throw on fires caused by incendiary bombs," they were telling residents of their district.

"Not a big job, either," I thought, "but it's a very necessary one, and they're getting it done. Everybody's doing something."

That night, Mrs. C——'s "ship's wives" properly accounted for to the last one, we clustered together, "fifteen of us—counting unborn babies—" as Mr. Frear said, sitting around the radio in the dark, asking each other questions which we could not answer.

"How did they do it? Did they get help from the local Japanese? Are the local Japanese out sabotaging? Have parachute troops really landed in Woodlawn and Upper Manoa, as we heard? Have they got the carriers? Will more planes come back tonight?"

As we each sought out our sleeping places, I realized that this had been the most exciting day in the history of Hawaii—and it has had some pretty glowing times. But I had seen and heard all too little. There were so many more things I wanted to know. My mind kept coming back to the Japanese. I remembered all the horror stories I had heard about yard men being prepared to cut off the heads of their employers. Absurd, but as I groped around in the dark I thought of Yamato and his efficiency. Ashamed to let anyone else know what I was thinking, I slipped downstairs and brought in the outside keys to the front and back doors.

I resolved to start the very next morning getting the story of what happened. I was going to talk to everybody I could who had seen the events of the day at first hand—to everyone from commanding officers on down to the lowliest seaman second-class, to the wounded, the unhurt, the heroes, and the anonymous workers whose collective response to duty was even more important than the feats of individuals, extraordinary as they were.

I got that story, and I shall never forget it. It was the most amazing I had ever heard. Nothing I could add to what these American officers and men told me could make it better. If emotion is here, it is because I have kept the words of the many men who did the deeds of heroism and who uncomplainingly suffered the wounds and agonies. The figures of speech are theirs, the restraint, and the lack of desire for an "effect."

Theirs is a plain, straightforward story, but if I have told it as I have tried to—that is, as it was given to me—it will make every man in America want to shoulder a gun and every woman wish to be a soldier's wife in this war.

# *At the Flying Fields*

IT IS NO military or naval secret that our air fields on Oahu are here to protect Pearl Harbor, America's "billion-dollar fist" in the Pacific. Wheeler Field, Hickam Field, the Naval Air Base at Kaneohe, the Marine Base at Ewa, were all built for a purpose and are an essential part of our defenses. All these are within quick flying time of the Harbor. Three are not more than two or three minutes apart when you are in a plane going three hundred miles an hour. Everyone knows this, and no one better than the Japanese who attacked on that fateful Sunday. They tried to ground every plane we had in order to prevent pursuit by our pilots.

It is believed that the Japanese approached from two directions almost simultaneously, coming in three waves from opposite sides of the island. Since the attacked areas are so close together, everything happened at once. By the time the first wave of attacking planes was approaching Pearl Harbor and neighboring Hickam Field, the second was already dropping bombs on Wheeler.

The method of attack on each air field was the same.

Small squadrons of mustard-yellow bombers with the blood-spot of the Rising Sun on their wing-tips flew in swift and low, bombing the hangars and strafing planes on the ground. While a Japanese plane dropped a well-directed bomb on a hangar, back and forth went its fellows, spraying the long orderly rows of super fighting planes with incendiary machine gun bullets. Hangars were left in ruins. Many of our airplanes burst into flame and were lost.

Our men everywhere were shocked but never panicky. Narrow escapes and heroic deeds happened by the score every second—so many that not all of them will ever be recorded. It was a sad day for America, and especially sad for us in Hawaii, but it was also a heartening day. We can be proud of a country that has such people in it.

## KANEOHE

The commanding officer of the Kaneohe Naval Air Base was having his breakfast coffee, grunting an occasional "Uh-huh" to his fifteen-year-old son's remarks about Superman. The commander heard planes in the direction of the Koolau mountains. He looked out the window and saw three flights of three planes each, flying low, and making a right turn into the entrance of the bay, where planes of the naval air base were moored.

"Those fools know there is a strict rule against making a right turn!" the commander exclaimed, leaping to his feet.

His son said, "Look, red circles on the wings!"

The first alarm was the screeching of the commander's automobile tires coming down hill to the administration building, his battle station.

The Japanese planes shifted into echelon formation —a straight row, one behind the other—as they zoomed over the quiet bay. They flew low, no more than fifty feet above the unruffled surface of the water. Below, planes lay anchored in the bay. A hundred yards away were the shifting crews of the anchored airplanes. Two boat loads of young seamen were passing each other. "Here comes Tojo!" one of the boys joked. The Japanese opened up. Machine-gun bullets spraying into the water made a wide lane of geysers that led straight to the two boats and the anchored planes. Incendiary bullets and tracers shot down. Some bounced off the planes in red streaks. Some went through the anchored planes and sizzled in the water. The planes went up in flames. A few of the boys escaped.

The Japanese flew on to the end of the bay, made a turn like the bottom of a figure eight, and came back. They were met with the fire of a single machine gun. An ordnance man had rushed into the armory as soon as the strafing started. He brought out a Lewis machine gun, which is a field-type gun on a fork ready to be placed on any raised platform. He set it up on a covered tin garbage can, took a lead of fifty to seventy-five feet on the plane, and started shooting. Nothing happened, but he kept on shooting.

The enemy echelon went straight for bombing planes on the ramp and strafed them mercilessly on their way over. They continued to the entrance of the bay, made the small loop of the figure eight, and came back again.

Heedless of the strafers, gun crews rushed out to salvage machine guns from the burning planes and set them up outside. Streams of fire converged upon the attackers. For fifteen or twenty minutes this strafing attack kept up, the line of planes going continuously up and down in the figure eight, crossing each time directly over the planes on the ramp. They got it going and coming. The attackers also found time to do a bit of incidental strafing of unprotected persons. They killed and wounded some civilians on the roadway. They blew the tires off the car of a major, returning with his wife and children from church.

During the lull which followed, Kaneohe Naval Air Base was the scene of more and faster activity than it had ever had before. Men commandeered all cars and drove them to staggered positions on the field so that if an enemy plane tried to land it would crash on a car. All anti-aircraft units were set in place. Civilian employees ran to help put out fires and salvage the burning planes. They repaired electrical lines and water mains, so that the utilities of the station were out of commission only a short while. Contractors' men leaped to the seats of their bull-dozers and pushed burning planes away from the hangars.

Twenty minutes and the Japanese were back, this time strafing and bombing. They attacked the contractors' men on their bull-dozers. They strafed the men moving the automobiles. They dropped a tremendous bomb on one of the hangars. They shot bullets three-quarters of an inch thick into the hurrying people on the ramp. One of these bullets went through a reinforced concrete wall a foot thick. It left a hole a sewer pipe could have gone through. Wounded people fell, but they did not cry out.

Everywhere the gallant fighters answered back, but the attackers were flying fast and were hard to hit. A gunner had no place but his shoulder on which to anchor his Browning air-cooled automatic. It was five times as heavy as a good shotgun, it kicked five times hard, and it hit him fifty times in five seconds. He bounced around on it like a ping-pong ball tied to a paddle. He may not have hit a thing, but he was in there throwing lead.

A bomb missed a hangar and fell on open ground. The concussion drew a row of riveted steel-sash windows three inches from a wall eighty yards away. Rivets flew from the wall. A hundred yards farther on the concussion knocked down the ordnance man at his gun. Bomb after bomb fell until the administration grounds five hundred yards away were littered with splinters from one to five pounds in weight. The ordnance man had his revenge. Coming straight toward him, flying low, just clearing the telephone wires, was a Japanese in a single-seat pursuit plane, strafing after the bombers, protecting them from attack. The ordnance man took less lead this time, pulled his trigger once, and pushed hard against the kicking gun, while it poured its burst of fifty bullets into the Japanese plane. Others were undoubtedly shooting at him too. Perhaps it was not the ordnance man who got him. He didn't care. The important thing was that the plane crashed on a knoll of ground near the water. One wheel bounced through a house; the motor landed a quarter of a mile away.

Another plane was downed in the waters of Kailua Bay. A great cheer went up from the watching crowd, sounding even above the roar of airplanes and machine guns. The rest of the planes flew on toward Ewa.

## THE MARINE BASE

The Marine Base, a new incompleted air base a couple of minutes by plane from Pearl Harbor, was attacked as viciously as if it were an armed fortress. The first wave of Japanese planes concentrated their fire on all aircraft on the ground. During the momentary lull which followed, marines rushed out and dragged unburned planes off the runway. They mounted free machine guns on them. There was no concealment or protection for these planes, and they were plainly visible to the attackers, but volunteers rushed to man the mounted guns. The brief lull was followed by a second attack more vicious than the first. Wave after wave of strafing planes swept across the field. Cannon and machine-gun fire churned the ground around the planes, and this time bombs sought out what bullets might miss. Every plane was a target selected for special attack. Yet the men stuck to their guns, pouring a stream of fire at each Japanese plane as it dove past.

Private Turner and Sergeant Peters were firing fast from one of these quickly improvised posts. Turner calmly handed ammunition to Peters, the gunner. A bomb fell not more than ten yards from the plane. Still they fired. Three of the mustard-yellow attackers came at once, pouring their heavy fire into the lone plane. Turner was struck by machine-gun bullets. He fell from the wing of the plane, mortally wounded . . .

Throughout the attack every man carried out his emergency duties, despite the heavy fire which the Japanese poured upon every corner and cranny of the field. The marines distributed the ammunition, cleaned and serviced the guns, made bombs ready for use, and in every spare moment got in telling shots at the enemy. Moving vehicles were the special targets of Japanese attack, yet drivers of ammunition trucks and ambulances made their trips to every part of the field without looking first to see if the sky was clear. Usually it was not.

Technical Sergeant William Turnage alone set up and manned a free machine gun in the midst of the hottest fire of the first wave of attackers. A Japanese plane swooped toward him. He held his machine gun on the plane. Gasoline suddenly spurted in streams from a dozen holes. The plane changed its course, spun into the woods a short distance away, and crashed in flames.

The marines have a one-man fire truck. In the midst of the first attack, driver Shaw spotted several planes that had been set afire by Japanese incendiary bullets. He climbed into his red fire truck and set out for the line to put out the fires. Strafers, attracted by the bright red truck, attacked before Shaw got half-way to the planes. They riddled the truck with machine-gun fire. Shaw kept on. Two more planes attacked him. Still he flew. He did not stop until a third wave shot the tires off his wheels. When an officer commented drily upon his driving into a hail of machine-gun bullets, Shaw said, "Hell, Lieutenant, I saw a fire, and I'm supposed to put 'em out."

A master technical sergeant, veteran of the World War and the Nicaraguan campaign, was in charge of a bomb-handling detail. The attack became especially heavy in his area. He calmly devoted all his attention to the task at hand, ignoring the strafing with complete disdain.

"Sergeant! Take cover!" an officer yelled across to him.

"To hell with the cover!" he shouted back. "I'm fifty years old. Get the kids under cover!"

His bomb load went right on to the line of operation.

## WHEELER

Lieutenants Welch and Taylor, sitting at the officers' club at Wheeler Field, saw the Japanese dive bombers swoop low over the ammunition hangar and drop their load. Sinewy steel and thick bastions of concrete were twisted and shattered from the high-power explosion. The lieutenants rushed outside, leaped into their car, and hit a hundred miles an hour on the way to a nearby air field where they had their planes on special duty. They did not stop to hear the size, number, or type of planes attacking, but grabbed their airplane orders from the interceptor control and dashed for their pursuit planes on the field.

They rose to battle and headed straight for a squadron of a dozen or more Japanese planes over Barber's Point. Their planes were armed with only 30-caliber machine guns. The enemy planes were near now, and the two lieutenants bent to the attack. Lieutenant Welch made for one. It was a two-man dive bomber.

The rear gunman was spraying lead at the attacking American, but Welch sat on the Japanese plane's tail and shot it down with one well-aimed burst from his three machine guns.

One gun jammed. An incendiary bullet hit his plane, passing through the baggage compartment behind the driver's seat. He climbed above the clouds and checked. The plane was not on fire. He dove through the clouds and returned to the attack. A Japanese plane was flying out to sea. He caught it, shot it down, and saw it fall into the broad Pacific below. His plane needed refueling, so he headed back for Wheeler Field.

Lieutenant Taylor's plane overtook his first victim so fast that he had to throttle back to keep from overshooting. He found his mark and the plane went down. During his second attack, the enemy rear-gunner nicked Taylor's arm. The bullet spattered when it hit the seat, and a fragment pierced the American's leg. He felt it, but paid no attention. He joined Welch in the return for refueling, and the two landed together.

Before Welch's gun could be unlocked or Taylor's wounds receive first aid, a second wave of fifteen Japanese planes swept in, flying low and heading for the two planes on the runway. Taylor had been advised not to return to the air because of his wounds. He leaped to his plane, took off, rising at high speed, and turned in a perfectly executed chandelle. The Japanese were on his tail. Welch, in the air behind them, swept fast upon

Taylor's pursuers and dove on the one most dangerous to his partner. The Japanese rear gunner poured lead into Welch's plane. Bullets struck the motor, the propeller, the cowling. Still Welch pursued like an avenging fury, letting fly with all his guns. The enemy plane burst into flames and crashed. Taylor escaped. Welch followed another enemy plane seaward, caught it about five miles offshore, and gave its two-man team an ocean grave.

These fighters were not alone. Other squadrons were in the air. In another part of the sky Lieutenant Harry Brown saw his friend Lieutenant Robert Rogers in a dog-fight with two Japanese planes. Brown singled out the one on Rogers' tail and began shooting. He got nearer and nearer to the Japanese plane, so close that he saw his bullets plowing into it from the belly to the tail. One of his guns jammed. He pounded it with his fist until the skin burst. The plane in front started wobbling, then shot into flames and crashed into the sea. Brown's throat was sore and his voice hoarse from yelling during the excitement.

An old-timer, Lieutenant Sanders, led a unit of four planes up through an overcast of six thousand feet. He saw a group of six Japanese bombing an air field. He signaled his men to the attack, taking the enemy leader for himself. Although the sun was behind Sanders' unit, the Japanese saw them and fled north. The unit came in fast, dived on the Japanese, and started firing. Sanders opened up on the leader. The Japanese plane smoked up, faltered, and fell into the sea.

Lieutenant James Sterling was hot after one of the enemy.

A Japanese plane was on his tail. Lieutenant Sanders closed in, but the attacker was already pouring bullets into Sterling's plane, and it burst into flames. The American continued to fight the Japanese plane ahead, and the four went into a dive—the Japanese in front, Sterling still firing at him, the second Japanese after Sterling, and Sanders following through. They plunged down into the overcast at an altitude of six thousand feet, all motors roaring at full speed. Only Sanders pulled out.

Lieutenant Rasmussen was in a dog-fight with a Japanese over the pineapple fields of Wahiawa. Each was desperately maneuvering to get on the other's tail. Bullets flew into Rasmussen's plane. His radio equipment fell to pieces before his eyes. The Japanese plane was fast, well-armed. Below, thousands of people who had evacuated their homes at Hickam and Ford Island, and thousands who had run outdoors at Schofield Barracks and Wahiawa stood anxiously watching the dog-fight, the most exciting form of modern warfare.

Rasmussen pulled up out of a fast maneuver. He caught the Japanese plane in his sights. He pulled the trigger of his 50-caliber machine gun. Tracer bullets ripped into the enemy plane. He held the deadly stream straight on the Japanese. When he quit firing, the plane was going down. All the anxious thousands broke into a great cheer of relief and pride when it fell to the ground in a burning, broken mass of wreckage.

When Rasmussen landed, he looked at his plane. The rudder was shot away, and the fuselage was as full of holes as a sieve.

The Japanese got full satisfaction from their visit to "the eagles of Wheeler."

On the ground at Wheeler men were running through dust clouds rising from the Japanese strafers' incendiary bullets that were ripping up the ground. Dive bombers were planting demolition bombs on the hangars. Just before this blitz started, Sergeant Bayham tore down to the supply house for a machine gun. He was breaking down a door when the supply sergeant, who was still thinking "practice," refused the gun and ammunition unless Bayham signed for it. By this time the door was down, and Bayham was dragging out a 50-caliber machine gun.

"I don't have time to sign for it!" he yelled.

When he finally mounted the gun, somebody cried out, "Hey, you can't fire that water-cooled gun without water!"

"To hell with the water–I haven't got any water!"

Staff Sergeant Benton joined him and fed the ammunition as Bayham pumped it at the approaching Japanese two-motored bomber. The gunner in the rear cockpit was shooting at them. Dust popped up around them. Their own tracer bullets told them that they were hitting the attacker. Holes were going into the plane. When it had passed and was a couple of hundred yards away, the plane shook like a dog shaking off water, circled jerkily to the right, and fell.

Oahu's defenders fought. They fought on the sea, in the air, and wherever men found guns to fight with. Two Japanese planes came strafing the streets of Wahiawa, a few miles from Pearl Harbor. At the sound of firing, a lieutenant and a sergeant in charge of a communications section grabbed automatic rifles and rushed out to the sidewalk. The two planes flew low, slowly and deliberately. They raked everything in their path with machine-gun fire. Puffs of dirt exploded as the bullets whipped into the earth. One plane, blazing away, swooped down toward the unprotected communications station. The Americans knelt, took a lead on the plane as if aiming at a duck, waited until it was within 150 feet, and emptied their magazines. The machine guns stopped firing. The plane went out of control. It slipped sideways and crashed in flames a hundred yards behind the communications post.

## HICKAM

At Hickam Field, the air field so near Pearl Harbor that it is virtually the same target, a long row of hangars and bombers invited the Japanese. The attack combined bombing and strafing. The enemy planes bombed the hangars and strafed the quarter-mile-long row of planes drawn up in front of the hangars in orderly parade formation.

A bomb-hit on a hangar announced the news to the thousands on the post. Men came pouring out from all nine wings of the barracks—men in slacks, men in shorts, some in their underwear only, some without anything on at all. What was going on? Another mock war? No, bombs! Everyone ran for his battle station.

Colonel Ferguson was in a building up the street from the hangar line. He ran out into the open, saw the damaged planes, and jumped into the gutter. While strafers bounced bullets off the road by his side, the Colonel crawled down the gutter to the line. There he directed the tactical squadrons who were arriving a hundred to a hundred and fifty at a time on the double quick.

"Disperse those planes!" was the order.

Up and back, up and back, the Japanese squadron was flying, strafing the airplanes on the wings. The men ran on heedless of the rain of bullets. Some of the men faltered and fell.

A general's aide was already on the line. He was trying to taxi one of the big bombers. Strafers had put one motor out of commission. It was no easy job to taxi such a heavy plane with only one motor going. He did it by racing the one engine until it pulled its side of the plane forward. Then he slammed on the opposite brake, which forced the other wing up. Wading and crawfishing along under enemy fire, he brought the plane across the landing mat to comparative safety.

While the fire department fought flames at the tail end of some of the planes, daring crew men jumped upon the wings, disconnected the engines, and pulled their eight or nine hundred pounds' weight to the edge of the apron. Fine engines were saved by their quick thinking.

Inside one hangar twenty-one Hawaiians were fighting fire. Planes roared hoarsely, machine guns stuttered overhead. In the middle of the smoke-filled hangar, Solomon Naauao, 245-pound athlete, trained the water from his fire-hose on the fuselage of a four-motor flying fortress, pushing back the gasoline fire that leaped out from the fuselage onto the wings. Solomon is a giant Hawaiian, a true son of a warrior. Short, thick, black hair fits his massive head like a fur cap. He was hoping the Chief would come soon with the foamite. Water was not much good against gasoline.

One end of the burning hangar fell through to the

floor, revealing a sky dotted with three approaching Japanese bombers. They were flying just a few feet above the hangar. The first one passed directly above Solomon and his fellow-fighters. Solomon heard an explosion and felt hot pain.

"Lord help me!" he prayed, falling to the concrete floor. The whole inner side of his right leg was blown away.

With his arms and sound leg he crawled through the smoke, away from the flames. When two soldiers picked him up, he learned that five others with him had been wounded, three more blown to pieces. They left him in the doorway to wait for the ambulance just coming in. As he lay there, Japanese planes flew slowly above, just clearing the hangar, and strafed the men running to carry him to the ambulance. Others quickly picked him up and sped him to the hospital.

Sergeant Dwyer got a machine gun out of ordnance, put a corporal in charge of it, and dashed back for another. A bomb fell, and its deadly fragments flew. He got his second gun and set it up on the parade ground. He felt wet and looked at his shirt. It was soaked with blood. The sergeant remembered that something he had thought was a stone had hit him when the bomb exploded. He was taken to the hospital with a shattered shoulder.

A lieutenant ran toward a plane. A Japanese flew

over, strafing. The lieutenant fell to the ground, mortally wounded. A young corporal by his side lifted him to an ambulance, sped back across the apron, leaped in the plane, and taxied it out.

The raid lasted fifteen or twenty minutes. As soon as it ceased, activity burst upon the streets and flooded them. Ambulances and all the cars that could be pressed into service as ambulances were whizzing up and back from the bombed area. School buses, army station wagons, American Factors delivery trucks, and private cars helped to deliver the wounded and to rush surgical supplies from Honolulu to the hospitals.

Before half their work was completed, they were caught in the second and most destructive raid. Two rows of high-flying bombers dropped over twenty heavy and light demolition bombs from a height of ten to twelve thousand feet. They landed in the most populous section of Hickam Field. For what seemed a full minute after the bombs had landed, there was a dead silence in which nothing happened. Then the new mess hall, large enough for six complete basketball courts inside, the photograph laboratory, the guard house, the fire station, the barracks built to house thousands, an immense hangar—everything in the entire area—seemed to rise intact from the earth, poise in mid-air, and fall apart, dropping back to the earth in millions of fragments and clouds of dust.

The third wave came strafing. Ground defenses were going full blast and accounted for several of the raiders. Guns were set up on the parade ground, on the hangar line, and even around the flagpole at post headquarters. One man—no one knows how—had lugged a machine gun up on top of one of the unbombed hangars and was perched up there, popping away at the strafing planes.

Green men under fire acted like veterans. All moved swiftly to their places without any confusion or disorder. The cooks ran back into the kitchen to remove all the stored food to a safer place. The kitchen was hit. The Staff Sergeant in charge was struck on the head by a piece of shrapnel. He ripped off his shirt, tied up his head to stop the blood, and went on directing the work.

Outside, a corporal was speeding across the parade ground to help man a machine gun. It was entirely in the open, without any protection whatever. Halfway there he was strafed by a low-flying Japanese pilot. Mortally wounded, he kept on, trying to get to the machine gun. He fell dead on the way.

His place was quickly taken. Eager privates ran out and took over the gun. They did this time and again, dashing out under fire and taking over free machine guns, even though the men who were operating them had just been strafed and killed.

On the apron opposite the hangars a lone man was firing a 30-caliber machine gun which he had carried out and set up on the mount of a B-18 bomber. It was unstable, because the mount was made for an aerial gun. He braced it against his shoulder and kept up a steady stream of fire. An enemy plane flew low, strafed the plane he was in with incendiary bullets, and set it on fire. There was no way for the lone machine gunner to get out of his position in the nose of the bomber. All behind him was a flaming death trap. Spectators not far away said that he did not even try to get out, but kept on firing. Long after the leaping flames had enveloped the nose of the plane, they saw the red tracer bullets from his machine gun mounting skyward.

There was humor with the tragedy. When the Japanese came over Hickam the third time, they placed a bomb squarely on the "Snake Ranch," the boys' name for their recently opened beer garden. A first sergeant of a truck company had endured the first two waves bravely enough, but this was too much. He dashed out of his barricade, shook his fist at the sky, and shouted, "You dirty S. O. B.'s! You've bombed the most important building on the Post!"

A group of U.S. bombers, all unarmed, were just flying in from the mainland when the bewildered pilots suddenly found themselves pounced upon by a fleet of armed and shooting bombers. Many of the Americans did not see the Rising Sun on the planes and simply could not imagine what had broken loose above their heads. What kind of Hawaiian welcome was this? The planes were to be delivered to one particular field, but they dispersed in every direction and landed wherever they could.

# At Pearl Harbor

ALL THAT HAPPENED at the air fields was only a prelude to the drama of Pearl Harbor. For years the Japanese have wanted to smash this Gibraltar of the Pacific. It stands in the way of any successful attack on the mainland United States. "If we could only 'get' Pearl Harbor," the Japanese militarists tell themselves, "we could raid the West Coast of the United States at will." And they could. Every detail of strategy in the attack showed that Pearl Harbor was the real objective. Planes were used in attacking it that never bothered to approach the landing fields. The attack lasted from 7:55 A.M. to 9:15 A.M. and there were probably 150 Japanese planes —torpedo planes, strafers, dive bombers, and high-altitude horizontal bombers.

I cannot tell you how many ships were lying in Pearl Harbor on that peaceful Sunday morning. That is a naval secret. I can tell you the names of the *Oklahoma,* the *Utah,* and the *Arizona,* because they have been mentioned in dispatches and in the newspapers. I cannot tell anything more specific. But you know that Pearl Harbor is the United States' largest naval base, and that its spacious waters can float every ship of any navy in the world. Battleships were there, those great warships named for the states in our union, anchored in the harbor. Destroyers lay near them, mine-layers, cruisers, and all the types of ships that the great navy of America boasts. On each were boys and men of the United States Navy from virtually every city and county of the forty-eight states, from towns with such outlandish names as Wahoo, Nebraska, and Hominy, Oklahoma.

A great surprise was in store for them, the greatest in their lives, and the most astounding in the life of the U.S. Navy. From somewhere, exactly where they did not know, a wave of torpedo planes flying in from the direction of Honolulu, swift, low over the calm waters of the Harbor, eased down toward the ships, and released their torpedoes, glittering like fish in the sun, plunging with a loud splash into the sea.

You can tell a torpedo plane by the way it approaches its target. It comes down at an angle, levels off, and drops its torpedo as near the target as possible. The Japanese squadron of torpedo planes came in two waves. Each plane had its object carefully selected in advance, or so it seemed, for the approaching planes separated and each went to a definite attack.

From the crow's nest of one of the battleships, a sailor saw one of the ugly mustard-colored planes heading toward the side of his ship. He saw its deadly "fish," like a great shark, propeller for a tail, splash into the water below. The plane roared upward, barely clearing the deck of the ship. The sailor, paralyzed by the horrible fascination of awaiting the inevitable, watched the wake of the torpedo, coming straight for his ship. Massive battleship, of thousands of tons, it rocked as if hit by a mighty fist. Almost simultaneously with the horrendous roar which accompanied the blow, quantities of oil flew all over the ship. The oil caught on fire. In two minutes the deck of the ship was covered with flames, as if it were an oil tanker that had been hit. Flames leaped as high as the crow's nest on which the lone sailor stood. Billows of heavy, oily smoke enveloped him. It was like sticking his head in a burning chimney flue to look over. Terrific heat, smoke, the gas from the bomb blinded and choked him. He fell to the floor of the crow's nest and hid his face in his arms. Cries of the burned and wounded below came up to him. He raised himself and tried to look down. Cinders and flakes of burning paint flew into his eyes and blinded him. Gropingly, he climbed upon the edge of the crow's nest and leaped into the oil-covered, flaming water below, just missing the deck. He swam under water as long as he could, then came up for breath. In a moment the burning oil forced him under again. It was only a short way to Ford Island, but when he clambered up on the beach, every hair had been singed from his head. Yet he went on fighting.

The captain of another ship was below in his cabin when the first explosion came. He leaped to the port-hole. The water, ordinarily eight or nine feet below, was only six inches from his face, and covered with oil. At that moment the ship was hit again. Water gushed into the cabin. He snapped the catch underneath the porthole just in time. As he did, the ship listed farther, and through the glass he saw the water come above the porthole. He turned to the door and heard the rush of water down the passageway. When he opened it, the torrent of water surged over the floor of his room. By the time he had fought his way to the top of the ladder, the whole compartment below him was filled with oil and water. He was like a rat caught in a sewer.

As the captain stepped out on deck, ready to run for his battle station, a bomber flying almost directly above him dropped an incendiary bomb. Instantly hundreds of fragments of red-hot steel were flying at him, and all over the ship. He leaped behind the combing of the hatch and was not hit.

In the next second a bomb hit, knocking one of the ship's airplanes from its catapult. As it crashed to the deck, one of its pontoons broke off and came hurtling toward him. It hit the hatch-combing behind which he crouched, and flew off into the water. It would have been death to move. To walk out now was to enter a wall of shrapnel and machine-gun fire.

This hell lasted until the first wave of airplanes withdrew—perhaps twenty minutes. Suddenly the noise ceased, and the captain could hear voices on the nearby shore of Ford Island. The ship was listing. The order came to abandon ship. Behind the hatch, on the side of the ship away from Ford Island, a young ensign and two enlisted men were struggling to release a life raft. It had been caught in the deck rigging, and they could not approach it from their side. The captain stepped up to it and, with that super-strength that comes in such moments, shoved it out. From the raft, the captain, the ensign, and the two men rescued others who had abandoned the ship and were swimming around in the oily water. Many of them were so completely covered with the heavy fuel oil that they could not open their eyes. Several were vomiting, sick from swallowing oil and salt water. While they were struggling at their rescue work, a Japanese plane, one of the second wave, swooped down and strafed them, but missed. The rescuers collected twenty-eight men and took them ashore to the Navy Yard, opposite Ford Island.

Hundreds were still on the ship. Among them was a young lieutenant, lying dazed on the deck. He and his men had been dogging down the hatches when the first torpedo hit, rocking them like peanuts in a bag. Fumes from the fuel oil mixed with ether from the medical supply room, which had been hit, overwhelmed them. Not knowing what was choking them, they ran to the forward compartment for gas masks. When they opened the door of this compartment, they found twelve or fifteen men, some standing knee-deep in oily water, some fainting and falling. The lieutenant and his men dragged these suffering fellows into the next compartment, but the passage through which they had to go belched such a quantity of fumes that the whole crowd were overcome, falling to the floor unconscious.

The young lieutenant came to on deck. He had been pulled out and taken aft. As he woke, a bomb hit the compartment they had just left. It was the most terrific explosion that had yet occurred. The concussion caused by thousands of pounds of TNT sent every loose thing on the ship flying. Paint was jarred loose from every part of the ship's deck and flew off as if hit by a thousand invisible chip hammers. The lieutenant's hair was filled with it. The heat ignited the fresh paint on a turret, which burst into flames. A lad was climbing an outside ladder. The concussion blew him into the iron rungs. His body came through on the other side in as many pieces as the sections he covered. One seaman was blown against a bulkhead. Identification was impossible.

The young lieutenant was rescued.

On the same ship, while the universe itself seemed to be exploding, a Negro mess attendant who had never before fired a gun, manned a machine gun on the bridge until his ammunition was exhausted. Then he dived over the side and swam ashore.

These were the scenes being enacted all over the Harbor. Thousands of men were leaping overboard from decks and portholes of battleships, cruisers, and all kinds of craft. Hundreds never came ashore. They were caught in their compartments. On one ship which was turning on its side, a young chaplain was standing by a porthole, working swiftly and silently, helping men through. The last one in the line was helped out. When it came his turn, it was too late. "Go ahead, boys. I'm all right!" were his last words.

A yeoman, seaman second-class, was filing liberty cards on the second deck inside the *Oklahoma* when the call came, in a calm tone, "Unengaged personnel lay to third deck!"

As he went down the ladder, the same officer's voice yelled to him through the loud-speaker system, "All hands to General Quarters! This is no s – – –! The Japs are attacking!"

The yeoman felt the ship jar and shake. He ran aft to the next compartment. The ship was listing. As he came out on deck by his battle station, holding on to the galley ladder to keep from slipping, he heard a man crying out. He turned and saw a seaman caught by a heavy door which had closed when the ship listed. The yeoman started to help, but as he let go his hold on the galley door, he slid down the side of the listing deck. He landed in three feet of water which had already climbed up on the deck as the ship turned over.

He climbed back to the door and helped the struggling seaman release himself. Both then began to pull themselves upward on the increasingly steep deck. Seamen by the hundred were clinging to the sides of the deck, all straining upward toward the "lifeline." The yeoman saw the chief commissary steward fall half a dozen times. The lifeline is three chains that run around a battleship as the iron railings do around a passenger ship. If they could make it to this lifeline, they could then slide down the hull of the capsizing ship and land in the water only a few feet from Ford Island. They reached the welcome chain, pulled themselves to it, and slid down the side to safety.

Possibly the most terrific series of explosions that the peaceful island of Oahu has known since the eruption centuries ago of the extinct volcanic craters of Punchbowl and Diamond Head occurred on the *Arizona.* A flight of horizontal bombers, flying high above their torpedo planes and their air bombers, at an altitude of ten to twelve thousand feet, dropped a series of armor-piercing bombs almost simultaneously onto the stationary vessel below. Their immense weight carried them through more than one deck before they exploded. One dropped like a plummet straight down the funnel and blew up the ship's forward magazine where ammunition was stored. Torpedoes and high-powered explosives joined the bombs. The inside of the whole forward ship blew up instantly. The after part of the ship shook as if it would fall apart like a stack of cards. The forecastle waved up and down. Turrets jumped into the air and came down again. Fire and smoke pushed up through the seams of the deck.

A great swishing sound, followed by a tremendous boom, accompanied the explosion. It was a strange sound to all ears, but every one of the thousands on the other ships and on shore knew what it meant . . .

Human beings on the ship were helpless. Bodies flew two and three hundred feet into the air, hurled about as tiny particles are whisked aloft in an uncontrollable fire.

A group of twenty men and officers were caught in a turret. All lights went out. A hot blast enveloped them in the darkness. They felt a pressure on their ear drums. Nauseating gas and smoke smothered them. All communication with the outside was gone—ship's service phones, battle phones, and high-power phones.

"What kind of gas is it?" a seaman asked, choking.

"Yes, what kind is it?" others asked excitedly.

There was confusion and danger of panic, but at one command, "Quiet!" not a word was spoken.

"Breathe through your clothes," an officer directed.

A seaman produced a flashlight, and with it they found their way through the thick smoke to the ladder. The man sent up to open the hatch took a long time. The men waited in the heavy smoke. Coughing became louder and louder. No one cried out, "For God's sake, hurry!" They waited like professional seamen. The hatch was opened and they got out.

They burst out upon an amazing sight. The forward part of the ship was a mass of shattered, burning wood and twisted metal. Bodies of the dead were thick on the deck, and some were hanging from the forecastle. Men were running out of the flames, falling on the deck, jumping over the side. Japanese planes were flying low over the ship, strafing the fleeing seamen and those huddled together under the turrets. A second lieutenant lay on his back with blood on his shirt front. A corporal running by bent over him, took him by the shoulders, and asked if there was anything he could do. The young lieutenant was too near death to answer.

Out of the chaos the men heard a voice of calm reassurance.

"Take it easy. Don't get excited. Leave the ship for Ford Island." They followed the instructions.

It was the voice of the ranking surviving officer, supervising the saving of the wounded. He went into the flames. Many who came walking out with him were so badly burned that they were barely able to stand. Clothes burned away, no eyelashes, no hair, they stumbled along, feeling their way, helpless, yet not a man of them uttering a groan or a cry.

One boy about twenty-one, with wide blue eyes, kept repeating, "I can't see. I can't see." The officer passed his hands in front of his staring eyes. They did not flicker.

The chief officer worked swiftly, surely, and took no shelter the whole time, coming out of the flames into machine-gun fire from the Japanese above who continued to strafe the wounded and dying. Wooden splinters flew from the deck around him, spattered by their bullets. Many of the wounded and some of those unhurt would have failed to get off the burning ship had it not been for his presence of mind and his unmatchable courage. Men took heart from his calmness, forgot about themselves, and turned to fight the fire or help others escape.

"When are you leaving, sir?" someone asked.

"Not until the Japs leave!" he answered through the flames.

"Abandon ship!" he cried, and the cry was taken up by all hands.

"Abandon ship! Abandon ship!"

Before they left, six or seven men opened all the hatches. One man below breathed the air of freedom again.

Many of the men in abandoning the ship leaped overboard, leaving their room in the boat for the wounded.

The oil was so thick on the surface that they could hardly swim. A marine major, struggling toward shore, saw a man who was going under. The major was very tired, knew they both would probably drown, but he grabbed the fellow's shirt and said, "Hold on to my shoulder!" A few yards farther on, the major floundered. The other (he was a corporal) loosened his grip.

"Make it alone, Major!"

The major grabbed the panting man by his shirt and held him up, refusing to let go until they both reached the beach.

The last thing the boys in the small boat saw as they pulled away with the final load of wounded was the ranking surviving officer, alone on the quarterdeck, the ship aflame from Turret 3 forward. When he had made sure that no one else was left alive on the ship, he leaped overboard and swam ashore.

The *Oklahoma* had turned over. The *Arizona* was lost. Flames were leaping up from the *Downes,* the *Cassin,* and others. Men were killed and wounded, dying on every air field, in Pearl Harbor, and in the streets of Honolulu. Airplanes, ships, and homes were afire, but the Japanese imperialists lit a new fire that day which, praise be to the allied armies, will sweep over the world, carrying democracy and liberation even to Japan's own people.

Even that day, the attackers got a taste of what is to

come. Once the first shock had passed, America swerved and hit back. From every part of the island, defense forces rose to action.

Before the attack, a seaman first-class was writing a letter near one of the machine-gun nests. When the first Japanese plane came over, he manned the machine gun and fired away, scoring several hits. He got his first plane before "General Quarters," the call to battle stations, was sounded.

In the wardroom of a 1500-ton destroyer, an Academy ensign and three reserve ensigns heard the announcement from the bridge telephone: "The *Utah* has been torpedoed by Japanese aircraft!"

Immediately they sounded General Quarters and manned their battle stations. As senior officer, the Academy ensign gave orders to get underway at once. One of the reserve officers took the bridge with the senior officer, another took the guns, and the third became damage-control officer.

Five minutes later they opened against the enemy with their machine guns. Japanese planes were diving at ships in the harbor. Two minutes later Ensign —— brought his large caliber anti-aircraft battery into action.

Below decks, the chief machinist mate, acting as engineering officer, lit off another boiler. Fortunately, they already had steam under one. The chief boatswain's mate led his repair party into the job of clearing ship for action.

Within a short time they were heading for the channel. A gun jammed. The chief gunner's mate ordered all his men away from the gun shield and out of the handling room. At the risk of being blown to bits, he cleared the jammed shell, called the men back, and continued firing.

As they moved downstream, they kept up a hot fire with their main battery and machine guns. Four planes went down in smoke. Two planes dived over the destroyer, trying to reach the battleships beyond. Machine guns got them.

Abeam Fort Weaver, the Academy ensign called for more knots. The chief gave them.

They sped out of the Harbor, heading for their area.

The chief radioman got a good contact on his listening apparatus.

"Submarine!"

They maneuvered the destroyer for the attack and dropped two depth charges. Then they regained contact and dropped two more.

A large oil-slick appeared on the sea and bubbles covered the surface for two hundred feet. At first they thought the submarine was surfacing, so Ensign —— trained the battery to starboard to be ready for it.

Suddenly a third contact was reported. Apparently the submarine was heading for a cruiser near by.

The destroyer made an emergency turn and attacked. From the racks the ensigns loosed another pair of depth charges. When they swung around again they saw another oil-slick. They had sunk a second submarine.

From then on they screened the cruiser. Though she had expended hundreds of rounds of high-explosive shells and thousands of rounds of machine-gun bullets, the destroyer's young officers returned her to Pearl Harbor without a single casualty.

Officers and men worked together and set each other inspiring examples. A first lieutenant of one ship exposed himself continuously to the enemy strafing while directing operations on the quarterdeck and boatdeck. He ordered men not engaged to keep back in sheltered areas, but he himself remained constantly exposed in order to direct the work of damage control and putting out fires.

His example was followed by the boatswain's mate, who was sent to the booth of the officer of the deck to phone the central engine room to put more pressure on the fire mains. While he was phoning, a bomb struck near the booth and enveloped him in flames. He stayed at the phone to get the message through.

An ensign on the same ship manned a three-inch battery until the ammunition supply was blocked by fire and water. Any place on a burning ship is dangerous, but the ammunition supply room is the most dangerous of all. Nevertheless the ensign organized a party of volunteers to go below. There they worked swiftly and silently, in constant danger of being blown to bits. They carried ammunition through the fire, supplying other batteries to fight off the Japanese. A bomb exploded, and the shrapnel flying from it mortally wounded the brave ensign. His men wanted to carry him above, but he ordered them to abandon him.

"It's too late to save me," he said. "Save yourselves!" He died by his post.

On every ship men leaped to their battle stations and poured out reprisal fire from anti-aircraft and machine guns. One of the ships hit began turning over; its fighting crew followed it around as it capsized, firing their guns until they went under water. They swam to the dock, cheering a more fortunate ship than their own as it cleared the harbor.

All guns were put into use. A country lad from the West, a lowly "boot-seaman," had a standard rifle shoved in his hand.

"Get out and shoot!" was the command.

A small dive bomber came in, poised to drop a bomb. The boy had not been trained to handle a heavy rifle, but he had "done lots of huntin' " in his day. He took a bead and fired. One of the freak accidents of the war occurred. Apparently the boy's bullet hit the detonator of the bomb the Japanese was about to drop, for the plane simply burst in mid-air and disintegrated before their eyes. The boy fainted.

On one of the ships, a chaplain robed in his ecclesiastical gowns was setting up his reader's stand in preparation for the morning service when a bomb explosion announced the attack. He dashed to the door where they were dealing out arms, and grabbed a machine gun. Using his reader's stand for a prop, he set up the gun and fired away, refusing to let go until the attack was over.

A chief gunner was lying in his bunk recovering from yellow fever shots. The first torpedo hit just forward below him. He was thrown to the ceiling, and landed with a wrenched back. Fuel oil was coming in. Forgetting his back, he ran to the magazine to help get anti-aircraft ammunition going up to his battle station. Men there were being overcome by fumes from the fuel oil, and were falling on the deck. A man sent to the phone to call for help was enveloped in the fumes and fell to the deck before he could reach the phone. The gunner took the phone and called the Sky Control.

"Men for the five-inch anti-aircraft!" he shouted.

He turned to the guns, but there was no more ammunition. He dashed back to the ammunition room. The floor was strewn with asphyxiated men. He started getting out ammunition himself, and fell to the floor in a faint.

The gunner woke that afternoon on a mess table in the marine grounds, his back hurting. He was naked. Rescuers had removed his oil-soaked clothes. He leaped from the table; ran to the supply room; got a shirt, shoes, and trousers; and returned to the ship.

Two marines were manning a machine gun. A Japanese plane flew low and dropped a bomb which exploded on deck. A burning fragment from it sank into the back of the marine firing. While his mate tugged at the jagged steel and pulled it from his flesh, the marine kept firing his gun at the attackers.

This was the real spirit of Pearl Harbor.

# Some Noncombatants

EUGENE BURNS, ASSOCIATED PRESS correspondent, heard the rumbling of guns, but went on with his breakfast until a bomb burst near by.

"Say, something's on!" he said to his wife.

In fifteen minutes they reached town from their Tantalus home. On the way down they had seen the fires at Pearl Harbor. Burns stopped his car on Alakea Street and dashed into the Mutual Telephone building.

"Associated Press, San Francisco! Number's Douglas 6575!"

He picked up more information and details from the telephone girls while he waited for the connection. He wondered whether there would be any answer. If the *Chronicle* had not altered its ways since he left, no reporter would be there at this hour on Sunday.

"Hello!" he yelled, "the *Chronicle?*" It was. A reporter had come in for his mail. "Swell! Listen, here's a *story!*"

While he was making his dramatic report (which was used by the March of Time to introduce their description of the war), a bomb fell on the Schumann Carriage

Company a block away, and the explosion was heard over the phone by the reporter in California.

As he left, the operator said, "I'll bet the mainland papers are going to exaggerate this!"

At Pearl Harbor, M——, a captain's yeoman, and his wife and daughter, were playing with the baby, who was sitting in the middle of the bed. They heard an explosion and decided to pull the bed over by the window, where they could watch the mock raid.

They looked down toward the end of the island. The whole thing seemed on fire. A plane roared swooping down over a warship in the harbor. A terrific explosion followed as the plane swooped up again.

"Roberta! run outside and get your brother," Mrs. M—— cried to her daughter.

Roberta ran down the walk to where her little brother and his pal were playing with a small wooden wagon which they had made. As they started back to the house, a plane flew low above them and spattered the sidewalk with machine-gun bullets. The little wagon flew to pieces on the lawn. . . .

M—— went to his post of duty.

A few minutes later a truck swept up to the house.

"Get out of the house! Don't bring anything! Hurry!"

Mrs. M—— and the four children were crowded into the truck of fleeing wives and children. A plane swooped down, strafing. A machine-gun bullet went through the floor of the truck between Mrs. M—— and her eight-year-old boy.

The wild ride ended at a dug-out, where some three hundred persons were collected in safety. From there they could see a dog-fight, probably the one between Rasmussen and the Japanese. Tensely they watched until the Japanese plane fell in flames to the earth. Then the whole crowd cheered.

Johnny Kelly, on duty as life-guard at Barber's Point Military Reservation, looked out over the small bay for fish. A freighter offshore made its slow way along. An airplane flew above it. Suddenly a geyser of water shot up directly behind the ship. A shell landed half a mile from the beach and exploded not far from an early swimmer. Johnny, his friend Erling Hedeman, and four other life-guards talked about calling up headquarters.

"That kind of war-play is dangerous for swimmers," Johnny said.

The boys climbed up on the water tank the better to see what was going on. Over Pearl Harbor, and out Schofield way, planes were rising like bees from a hive suddenly stirred.

A shell landed on the beach near the water tower, blowing up a kiawe tree and leaving a hole about six feet deep. The boys scurried down and collected about ten pounds of shrapnel. It was so hot they could not hold it.

They cooled the shrapnel and carried it over to Erling's car, watching a formation of planes that appeared. Suddenly one of the planes left the group and dived for them.

"Slick model," Johnny was saying, "look at that N-line engine."

"Hey, look! The Rising Sun!"

When the plane had swooped down so near that they could see the rivets in its side, the Japanese pilot opened fire—pop, pop, pop, pop—all around them. Straight from the propeller the red tracer bullets came for them. Hot lead spattered on the macadam pavement at their feet. One bullet grazed Johnny's head, touching him just lightly enough to leave a pink crease across his brow. The plane swung up and away.

The six boys jumped into the car and started for a safer spot—they thought. Three Japanese planes, attracted to the target, dived for the car. The machine-gun bullets rained upon them. Six husky lads tried to disappear through the floorboard.

Erling raced at sixty in second gear down the highway. He was driving from the floor, and was so crowded he could not shift gear.

Zig-zag they flew down the narrow macadam roadway.

The planes closed in on their tail. Bullets peppered their fenders and the body of the car. They sounded like rocks hitting a zinc washtub.

On the right of the road a clearing appeared, leading

to a mango grove. They swerved off the highway and found refuge under the trees.

The car was riddled with holes. The gas tank was punctured, and gas was pouring out. The windshield was shattered.

The boys walked over to the beach, and on the way stopped at the weatherbeaten, two-room shack of Nick, the Hawaiian. His feet propped up on the wall of his porch, Nick was reading an old detective magazine. Without taking his feet down, he said,

"Hey, whassamatta, whassamatta? I live on dis beach forty-fi' year I never hear so much noise. No can read anymo'. I think bimeby I move from here!"

James Duncan is an amateur flyer, and belongs to the flying club, Hui Lele. There are twenty members who take time about with a plane. He had signed up for it on Sunday in order to get some instruction from Tommy Tomerlin, who gives lessons to the Hui Lele members when he can find time from his duties as co-pilot for Inter-Island Airways.

In compliance with club rules, the two men wrote down the time they left the airport: 7:55. Taking their time, they flew past Pearl Harbor, over the orderly flying fields of Hickam and Wheeler, and landed at Haleiwa, making a few practice landings there. They flew on to Kahuku and made some more landings on the emergency field there. Continuing on their way around the island, they passed over the Mormon Temple, famous show place, and admired it from the air. They had just flown over it when hell broke loose. Streams of red lead suddenly came cutting across them from two directions.

Two planes were attacking them, one from above in front, one from above at the side. The one from the front was diving on them. Red tracer bullets were shooting at them, some hitting the cockpit and cutting through the fuselage. The first attacking plane swept past the tail of their plane. It was followed immediately by the second attacker, which passed just over them. Their little "cub" plane trembled and shook in the wake of the swift, heavy bombers.

In the excitement neither Duncan nor Tomerlin had identified the planes. The only explanation for the attack that they could think of was that they might have flown too near a military reservation, and were getting a warning. It seemed a bit severe, especially when they saw that the first plane had made a chandelle and was heading for them again, tracer bullets flashing in a line from the attacking plane toward theirs.

In the next five minutes they were attacked three times, by both planes. When they finally did see the Rising Sun on the wings and tails of the planes, Tomerlin headed as fast as he could go for the steep mountain cliffs that follow the sea a part of the way on this side of the island. Flying very low above the water, only about fifty feet, and very close in to the jagged edge of the mountainside, they found cover.

The Japanese bombers were so heavy and fast that they did not have sufficient distance in which to attack and still come out of their dives.

They approached the Kaneohe air base, flying out to sea in accordance with military regulations as they passed it. Clouds of black smoke hung in the air above the base. Geysers of water were leaping into the air from fifty to a hundred feet, thrown up by bombs aimed at planes anchored on the water.

The two men wanted to head straight across the mountain range for home, but it was not a clear day, and clouds were hanging low, in some places halfway down the mountainside. Then they saw a triangle of light shining through a gap. They gained altitude and headed for the triangle. They forgot all warnings and flew close to the ragged edges of the cliffs. On any other day they would have considered that hitting the triangle was a delicate flying problem. Now they entered it boldly, skimming along only eight or ten feet above the tops of the guava bushes in order to avoid going into the cloud above. The violent air currents of the pali gave them a fillip and sent them on their way.

Once through, they came upon the whole panorama of the Japanese attack. Airplanes in formations of fourteen or fifteen winged their even flight over Pearl Harbor. Bombs like glittering schools of silver fish came raining down. They fell swiftly, steadily. A great rumbling shook the earth, and tremendous clouds of black oil smoke shot upward.

Stray planes were having it out in dog-fights over the sea. Other strays were circling and strafing the airports. Hickam and Wheeler showed the effects of the raid. Chaos had taken the place of the order which Duncan had admired on the way out an hour before.

As they approached their home field, the John Rodgers Airport, they saw that it was being strafed by enemy planes. The landing ground was cleared. All the planes were spread out to the four edges of the airport, spread wide apart. They were afraid to land, but they wanted no more attacks from the air, so down they went.

As they circled to land, a car rushed out of the hangar where they kept their plane. It reached them just as their wheels touched, and, racing alongside their plane, the driver of the car screamed, "Park that thing in the weeds and run for your life! The Japs are attacking us!"

Tomerlin ran the plane to the outer edge of the field and stopped. The two leaped out and started running for the hangar, directly across the open space. Duncan suddenly stopped, turned, and ran back to the plane for his hat.

Inside the hangar they were nervous, and decided it would be safer to get off the air field entirely. They ran for their car and set out in it down the road leading to the main highway. But the Japanese were strafing roads leading to the port; so they abandoned the car. They dove under a house just as a Japanese strafing plane shot across the sky above them. Shingles flew from the roof, knocked off by the machine-gun fire.

Duncan and Tomerlin crawled out and started home on foot. Down the highway they were picked up by a truck and taken in to town.

On Monday Duncan's telephone rang. It was the secretary of Hui Lele.

"Say, Duncan, you're being fined, you know."

"No. Why?"

"You didn't check in the time when you and Tomerlin got back to the airport yesterday."

There were at least three Hawaiians whom the Japanese literally did not disturb in the least.

The wife of a Navy officer at Ford Island is a very good painter. Her husband was away on duty. She had a picture to finish, and she was working on it so intently on Sunday morning that she did not notice that the "practice" bombing was being done by our neighbors from Tokyo. All through the raid she painted. If the truck driver whose duty it was to evacuate wives and children from her block stuck his head in at the door and yelled at her, she did not hear him.

The next afternoon she went out for a walk. A patrol guard stopped her.

"What are you doing here?"

"I'm taking a walk."

"You know we can't permit anyone to be here!"

"Why not?"

So it went until she discovered that she had painted through the most terrible catastrophe suffered in the Hawaiian Islands in over a hundred years—without knowing it.

The biggest news story of the year was on the wires. Harlan Reynolds heard it in New York over the radio. He picked up the telephone and dictated a cable to his maiden aunts at Waikiki.

At eleven-thirty the same morning it was delivered to them.

DEEPEST SYMPATHY DEAR AUNTS PLEASE COME HOME IMMEDIATELY.

"What in the world is the matter with Harlan?" they asked each other in bewilderment.

The news had made headlines in the New York papers, but it had not reached the ladies at their knitting in Waikiki.

# *The Wounded*

THE FIRST CASUALTIES to come in were those who were able to bring themselves. Men covered with oil and burns straggled ashore. A captain was with them, oil-covered, most of his clothing torn off. His admiral and superior officer had been killed. Just before the wounded stragglers reached the Naval Hospital, a Japanese bomber with three men in it fell from the sky, bounced off the concrete hospital building, cut a palm tree in two, and crashed in flames on the asphalt tennis court.

In the hospital, convalescents were hastily evacuated to temporary quarters outside to make room for the injured men who began coming in on stretchers. One young seaman had been hit on the side of the head above his ear by a piece of flying shrapnel. It drove into his skull behind his right ear and came out above his eye—out of his skull, but not his head. Lodged beneath the unbroken skin of his forehead, it bulged like a great bump. Incidentally, a machine gun had sprayed his stomach with lead. "We'll do what we can," the doctor said. The young seaman is alive to tell the tale.

Another youthful sailor came walking in with his whole lower face shot away—no upper lip or chin. He wanted to shake hands with everyone. He tried to talk, but his tongue only made noises against the roof of his mouth. "We were there together, fellows," is what he wanted to say. They buried him two days later.

Now the ambulances arrived. In they came, bringing the crippled, the burned. Swiftly, carefully, the litter bearers and the ambulance teams worked. They saved the lives of countless wounded by bringing them in during the "golden hours" before infection set in. Many a mother at home has these anonymous people to thank.

Numbers of young seamen had lost arms or legs, but hundreds were burned—burned from the sheets of flaming oil which had enveloped them on the battleships, and burned again from the lake of fire into which they had dived.

The spirit of these boys was unbelievable. The most impressive fact about the hospital, filled with wounded, many suffering unto death, was the silence of the place. No confusion, unnecessary clamor, no crying out. You never heard "Oh, that *hurts!*" They said, "Watch that leg, please, ma'am. It's broken in two places." Neither nurses, chaplains, nor doctors heard a murmur of complaint.

In an hour boys had become men, and men heroes. The medical officer walked down a row of wounded to select the one to receive immediate treatment. His trained eye at once saw the worst case. He went directly to a young boy. Burned skin was dripping off the youth's entire upper body.

"Take care of my buddy, here, Doc," the boy said. "He's hurt lots worse than I am."

That sentence was spoken more often than any other throughout the day—"Take care of my buddy." Boys who were much worse off than their neighbors asked nurses for water for their buddies, and said to the chaplains, "Padre, see if you can't find a doctor right away. My buddy's in terrible shape. He's been lying here ten minutes now."

The Naval Hospital was filled in a hurry, overflowing to the outdoors, to the city and plantation hospitals, until every available cot, nurse, and doctor was busy. While the strafing continued, Chaplain Strauss set up a seventy-five-bed emergency hospital in an unfinished barracks near the harbor. As each wave of planes came over, the attendants dropped to the floor. Tensely the men and women worked. Another wave came, and all went down, Chaplain Strauss with them. In the silence they heard a terrific rip. It was the knee of the Chaplain's trousers. When there was a lull, he rang up the Supply Department and told them to leave a needle and some thread the next time someone came by. Soon a special worker came flying with five hundred spools of thread and a hundred needles.

"Hey," one of the wounded men said, "whaddye think the padre wears, a tent?"

The Army wounded were taken to Tripler, the Army hospital. A Japanese bomb had made a direct hit on a mess hall at Hickam while three or four hundred young aviators were seated there, laughing and wise-cracking, having breakfast. Now maimed and bleeding, they were carried into Tripler. Dr. King put in an emergency call to the doctors of Honolulu for surgical teams. Again, the spirit of these American boys was thrilling to see. Their wounds were even worse than those of the burned. Some of them were too terrible to describe. They were mortal wounds by the side of which the loss of an arm or leg was nothing. Some had their chests or stomachs blown away. But all the time the ambulance teams and litter bearers were bringing them in and while they waited together for treatment, not one moan or whimper escaped them.

The doctors were amazed and inspired by the sight. In cases of this sort, they are accustomed to hear the most agonizing shrieks and groans. They expected a mad-house. They found boys living up to the code of professional soldiers—lie still and cause no more disturbance than necessary. They were not unconscious. They were alert, calmly waiting, and fully conscious of what they had gone through. There was not even any profanity. Nurses and chaplains moved among them, comforting the wounded and attending the dying.

A nurse put her hand behind the head of a blond boy of twenty, who had a serious chest wound, touched his lips with a glass of water. He took a swallow, smiled into her eyes, and said, "Thank you." They were his last words.

If spirit was high in the waiting line, in the surgical wards it was heroic. The whole experience of the morning seemed to act as a powerful anesthetic. The men did not seem to know that their bodies were hurting, undergoing such pain as often kills people from its shock alone. They were just out of action.

"Are you afraid?" the surgeon often asked.

"Not at all. Go ahead!" was always the reply.

One man said, "Just hurry up. I want to get back to my battle station!"

In three operating rooms, seven tables took the place of the usual three. Every table was kept busy, so that no time was lost. The medical officer moved swiftly among the cases, designating the order in which they should be treated. Hospital corps men and nurses were constantly on the lookout for means of accelerating the movement of patients into and out of the operating room. All was quiet and non-theatrical. It was the silence of courage.

The surgeons were grateful for the identification tags around each boy's neck, showing, among other things, his blood type. Precious time was lost whenever a patient had to wait to have his blood typed so that transfusion could be made. These boys *needed* plasma. They were so seriously wounded that they were as likely to die from the shock as from the wounds themselves. In such cases, a patient will be talking, and suddenly die. Shock is not fully understood, but doctors know that it is in some way related to the loss of blood. At Tripler, the surgeons pumped quarts and gallons of rich, life-sustaining blood into the veins of the soldiers, relieving them from the shock of their wounds and preparing them for the coming shock of surgery.

On young Lieutenant M——, there was no time to make a finished amputation, carefully moving the skin back above the line of amputation and then folding it over the stump when the operation was completed. His leg had to have attention, quick. Dr. Halford made a straight guillotine amputation, the kind that leaves a big stump and painful nerves exposed. When the stout lieutenant came back to have the wound dressed, a most painful operation, he tightened his lips, held on to the table, and stood the pain without a murmur. His example was repeated many times.

# Blood Bank

WE LEARNED IN Honolulu that Sunday how narrow the dividing line is between the soldier and the civilian in war time. We were inspired by the example of America's courageous soldiers and sailors, and fighting mad at the Japanese invaders for their cowardly attack. We wanted to do something. There was vitally important work to do, and civilians leaped to it.

Soon after the bombing started, a call came into the headquarters of the Hawaii Medical Association. It just said, "Pearl Harbor! Ambulances! For God's sake, hurry!"

This was the challenge that the Medical Corps had been waiting for from the day, months ago, when they first organized. And did they pick it up! Within only twenty minutes from the time the call came, the doctors and volunteer workers of the medical units had stripped the insides of over one hundred laundry trucks, lumber trucks, and delivery trucks of every description, equipped them neatly with previously prepared frames containing room for four litters each, and were speeding to the scene of action. One unit arrived early enough to receive a souvenir piece of shrapnel, flung at them by a Japanese bomb.

Another call came: "Department Surgeon King, at Tripler Hospital! Surgical teams, quick!"

Then occurred one of life's breath-taking coincidences. At that very moment virtually every surgeon in Honolulu was listening to a lecture on war surgery. It was being delivered by Colonel Moorhead, famous authority on the subject. The audience departed in a body for Tripler. In fifteen minutes, more capable surgeons stood ready at Tripler than Surgeon King could use.

By another coincidence no less fortuitous, they had with them a new surgical instrument which Colonel Moorhead had brought to Honolulu to demonstrate. Its purpose was to locate metal in the body and outline its exact location. The only instrument of its kind in existence, it proved its worth at once that morning. It saved precious hours of time that would have been spent waiting for X-ray pictures to be developed.

Colonel Moorhead, by the way, is Chief Surgeon on James M. Landis' Civilian Defense staff. He says he is telling him that "if you want to know how to organize civilian defense, come to Honolulu."

When the shooting started, Mrs. William Moir, chairman of the American Red Cross Motor Corps, was in it. She was swimming at Punaluu on the other side of the island when machine-gun bullets splashed the water around her. She looked up and saw a dog-fight going on in deadly earnest directly above her. She ran ashore. As she slammed the door behind her, a plane with the Rising Sun on its wing-tips fell into the deep water offshore.

When Mrs. Moir reached town, her motor corps was hitting on all eight. Seventy to one hundred women were out on the road. Every available sedan, roadster, and banana wagon was carrying men to Pearl Harbor. Driving on this three-lane highway was no job for a weakling. It has been almost a bottleneck of traffic ever since travel to and from the defense areas has put such heavy demands upon it. On that memorable Sunday it was an inferno. Army trucks, official and unofficial emergency wagons, ambulances, Red Cross cars and hundreds of taxis and Motor Corps women rushing officers and men to their battle stations literally screamed up and down the six-mile road.

The Motor Corps women were equal to the task. One member was on duty so early and rushed to the job so speedily that her car stopped a piece of shrapnel on its first trip out.

Dr. Pinkerton, making his rounds at Queen's Hospital, heard a commotion below in Emergency. He stepped to the balcony and looked down. Dozens of cases were coming in all at once—mutilations and burns. As the Doctor rushed back into the hospital to give instructions, an emergency call came from Tripler Hospital.

"Blood plasma, quick!"

In five minutes Dr. Pinkerton was at the refrigeration plant of the Hawaiian Electric Company where the local blood bank was stored. There were 210 flasks of 250 cc. (a half-pint). He rushed sixty of these to Queen's Emergency for the civilian cases coming in and sped on to Tripler with the rest.

The call came from Pearl Harbor: "Plasma!"

The precious fluid was divided and part hurried to the surgeons at the Harbor. It was going fast.

At eleven o'clock Dr. Pinkerton made a short appeal over the radio. He did not say how badly plasma was needed. He did not explain what it is, or tell how a young lieutenant's life had just beeen saved by its use. After getting his breath from running up three long flights of stairs at KGU, all he said was, "A call for volunteer blood donors! Report immediately to Queen's Hospital!"

In half an hour five hundred people were waiting at the doors of the hospital. The staff of doctors and trained technicians, some fifteen in all, were at work at twelve tables, but they could not take the blood as fast as it was offered. Some persons stood in line for seven hours to give their blood. Most of them did not know what blood plasma is, but they knew that they were helping.

The crowd of blood donors was a thrilling mass response to the dastardly Japanese attack. This waiting line was an amazing thing. Here were Honolulu's masses, a unique amalgam in the history of the world—a people who do not communicate with each other except on the level of pidgin English, but a people emotionally united. Honolulu society women stood in line or sat on benches by the wall beside the city's great good-humored lower classes. A well-known woman painter, a wife of a corporation president, and a waterfront washwoman waited together and talked about "what a treacherous thing it was." Japanese by the hundreds were there, many of them members of the Oahu Citizens for Home Defense Committee. Some older, alien Japanese were there too, dressed in black, which they traditionally wear on occasions where respect is due. They stood in attitudes of infinite patience, waiting to register a silent protest with their blood. A Portuguese blind boy of nineteen and his blind sister three years younger were there, brought in by their mother. They had heard the call over the radio and insisted that she bring them down.

Defense workers came in their dirty work clothes, got preference in the line, gave their blood, and went back to work. Welders came with eyes red and burning. They gave their blood, and back they went to the job. Large groups of employees came straight from work in busses provided by the companies. The beds had to be draped with newspapers to save the sheets from oil, canefield dirt, and the red soil of the pineapple fields with which the workers were covered.

A bunch of huge Hawaiians came lumbering in from the Honolulu Iron Works. Dirty and oily, when they leaned against the wall, they left big smudges. They were all taken into the same room for their lettings. They laughed and joked, teasing a Puerto Rican among them who was scared. "Wait till you get that shot of brandy at the end of the line, boy. You feel numba one swell!" they told him. The average extraction was about 400 cc., or something less than a pint. Several of these Hawaiians gave 750 cc. and went back to their job at the Iron Works.

A Dutch ship was in port for only a few hours. The entire crew came up to give their blood. Numbers of passengers came, too. Six big husky Dutch women came in a body. They were very welcome, for one of the things the doctors discovered was that a pint of woman's blood gives more plasma than a pint of man's. The Dutch sextet yielded generous quantities of plasma-rich blood.

Whole families came at once. The preferable age limits were from eighteen to fifty, but young boys lied and old men asserted their rights in order to be included in the line. The Hon. Walter F. Frear, former Governor of the Territory, and Mrs. Frear went down. He is seventy-eight and she is seventy-two. When it was suggested that they might be too old, Mrs. Frear said, "It ought to be very good blood. It has lasted us a long time!" "I should say so," said Mrs. Sarah Wilder, grandmother of grown men. "My blood is better than that of half of these young squirts!"

To the hospital came a letter by special messenger from a woman of eighty-one. It said in effect: "I realize that I am eighty-one, and that the request was for younger people. I am strong and healthy. However, I am very heavy and cannot stand long at a time without great fatigue. It will save me two trips to the hospital if you will permit me to make an appointment. My daughter will bring me down." And she added, "I may say that from what I have seen of this war so far, it is nothing like as bad as Custer's was in '76."

There was one Hawaiian woman who was so big that the doctors had to give up. In the depths of fat they could not find her vein. One seaman's wife had veins too small, and was rejected. Corps of Honolulu police and firemen made up for these, swelling the bank with averages well over 600 cc. each.

At the end of the line each donor who wanted it was given a generous shot of good brandy. The policemen accused each other of coming in because of the finishing draught. The beach boys pretended to be quite faint and were given long generous draughts to revive them.

A surprising number of girls who are following Sadie Thompson's footsteps in the South Seas showed up in the line. And four of them, after donating their blood, asked to help further. They got a job washing tubing, the dirtiest, smelliest, meanest of all laboratory jobs. They worked hard and stayed at it as long as anyone.

Many donors came back. One second-class seaman was recognized by a nurse.

"You shouldn't come back so soon," she warned him.

"My brother was killed," he said. "I want to do something."

That's what everyone in Hawaii is saying—"I want to do something."

# The Dead

EACH AFTERNOON FOR days the dead were buried. They died the deaths of heroes and were buried with the rites of the brave. They were buried simply and with dignity, without crowds of onlookers. The first was laid in the peace and quiet of Nuuanu Cemetery above the harbor where they fought. On each grave was a small bouquet of flowers—poinsettias, golden asters, and the many-colored island hibiscus. Golden sunlight spread out on the broad green lawn. Shadows lengthened fast, telling of the night.

An even row of tight-lipped, khaki-clad marines, their eyes fixed on the distant hills, stepped forward, raised their rifles, and fired three volleys over the graves of the glorious dead. A marine bugler sounded Taps. "Lights out. All quiet. Night has come." The clear notes of the bugle echoed through the quiet valley, a valley of legend and song, where happy people have lived in peace and freedom for over a hundred years.

A Catholic priest in black robes hallowed the ground with water. A Protestant chaplain blessed it with the committal ceremony. No one else was there. No loved one knew. No mother, wife, or sister away on the mainland could come to them. Later, after the war is over, they will be lifted out again and buried in cemeteries in their home towns on the mainland. Until then they are here in a pleasant green valley, looking down upon the sea.

There have been burials every day since, most of them at the new Navy cemetery at Red Hill, called Halawa, until over 2500 American soldiers and sailors killed in the surprise attack have been laid to rest in Hawaiian soil. Most of these funerals, like the first, have been unattended except for the marine firing squad and the chaplains. On New Year's Day Honolulu paid its respects to the dead in a memorial service at Nuuanu. Services were for over 350 sailors who lost their lives at Pearl Harbor and for three Hawaiian firemen killed at Hickam Field.

Several hundred persons attended, each wearing a flower lei in honor of the dead. They gathered around the ten long, wide trenches in which rows of men who had fought side by side now lay side by side, each in his own coffin. There was not a dry eye in the assembly as six part-Hawaiian girls sang the slow, sweet strains of "Aloha Oe"—"Until we meet again"—the saddest song ever sung at a funeral. The crowd stood with heads bare and bowed as a native Mormon missionary prayed.

Hawaiian women dressed in black, wearing leis of yellow feathers, laid long leis the full length of the graves. These were the Daughters of Hawaii, many of whom were descendants of warriors who fought and died long ago in this same valley.

Fleet Chaplain Macguire spoke with respect and anger in his firm voice:

"Let no one think they died in vain. Our 130,000,000 Americans would glow if they had seen how our boys died.

"They manned their guns until the decks buckled under them from the heat. Not a whimper. Not a moan.

"It was glorious!

"Don't say we buried our dead with sorrow. They died manfully. They were buried manfully. And we will avenge their deaths, come what may!"

# *The Japanese Community*

BY THE MORNING of the second day I was again able to view the Japanese in their true perspective, and I felt thoroughly ashamed of myself.

"I have lived in Hawaii since 1930," I thought. "Surely I can trust my judgment. Anyway, I don't have to trust it. Experts in the FBI and in the Army and Navy Intelligence services have told us not to get any foolish, hysterical ideas about the local Japanese."

Nevertheless, I wanted the latest word.

I found the palm-guarded Dillingham Building, home of the FBI, a chief center of interest. Onlookers were seated in the lobby, watching the round-up of suspicious characters. I joined them.

Three soldiers brought in a couple of Filipino boys. These prisoners were pretty harmless-looking specimens, tousle-headed, their shirt tails sticking out, but the soldiers stalked them as cautiously as if the prisoners might pull out bombs and throw them at any minute. I thought the Filipinos had probably been guilty of violating the blackout last night. This is a serious offense, so serious in fact that the police have orders to shoot out lights if their first warnings are ignored. These Filipino lads may have been playing, but the FBI does not consider pranks in order just now.

Mr. Shivers stepped out of the elevator. He is a quiet, brown-eyed man from Ashland City, Tennessee, who does not live up to his name. There is neither detective glamour nor flatfoot crudeness about him. He would more readily be taken for a fashionable doctor than a man quick on the draw. Since December 7, he has been co-ordinator of intelligence staffs in the Territory, and has been busy day and night directing the rounding-up of certain aliens and the questioning of suspects. I had a Coca-Cola with him at the Cafe Pierre next door, but saw that he was too busy to talk, and so did not attempt to ask him anything about the work. He remarked that Shunzo Sakamaki was with them now, that things certainly had happened fast, hadn't they?

I went back with him and we took the elevator to the second floor. Things had changed since I was there last. The Honolulu Chamber of Commerce office, facing the elevator, looked the same, but the hallway leading to the FBI offices was lined on each side with army cots the way the corridors of the legislative office building in Washington are frequently lined with desks. A soldier wearing a steel helmet and holding his bayoneted gun across his body, stood guard. Mr. Shivers left me and went down the narrow alley-way between the cot-rows to the conventional frosted doors bearing the sign FEDERAL BUREAU OF INVESTIGATION.

While I stood there talking with one of the Chamber of Commerce men who was leaning against the entrance door, several persons came out of the elevator, were challenged by the guard, and either passed on or stood waiting. One man seemed obviously a part of the organization—he had on a helmet, carried a gun, and looked as if he had been up all night, but he had to wait until someone from the office came out and said okay. A good-looking red-haired woman of thirty-five or so approached from the elevator. The guard, a boy of about twenty-one, blocked her way, looking a bit sheepish the while, as if ashamed of all the formality. She did not produce the proper credentials, however, and so did not get by. A Filipino man in overalls and shoes dirtied with the red mud of the pineapple fields wandered toward the guard as if lost. The guard gripped his gun and said, "What do you want?" "Down," the Filipino said, "down." "There," the soldier said, pointing with his bayonet to the elevator, which had stopped to let out some more passengers. The Filipino got on it and went down.

Following my clue, I returned to the lobby to wait for Shunzo Sakamaki, until he joined the FBI a professor of political science and history at the University of Hawaii.

In a few minutes a crowd of fifteen or twenty newsboys and other onlookers preceded some soldiers into the expansive lobby. Five soldiers, looking very grim and alert, used their bayonets to guide three Japanese men to the elevators. This case looked more serious than any of the others I had seen. One of the soldiers was carrying an armful of batteries, and another had a coil of wire. For nearly two years there has been a law in Hawaii against the use of radio sending sets, so that there is a lot of explaining to be done when one is found. The Japanese, in clean shirt sleeves, looked like well-to-do businessmen. They were very calm. Although they might have been innocent, they looked like men who would first do what they thought they had to and then take the consequences.

Shunzo came in. He is the quiet, steady type of Japanese, the kind who make good surgeons. He has come into prominence as the president of the Oahu Citizens' Home Defense Committee, the most active committee of the Major Disaster Council, and one made up almost entirely of Japanese-Americans.

Shunzo and the organization of which he is president are representative of the new methods adopted recently by the Army and Navy Intelligences, and the FBI. Hawaii offers these bureaus a special problem in espionage technique. Oahu is the chief defense outpost of the United States. Yet the territory harbors a population of 155,000 Japanese who could seriously embarrass, if not defeat, the islands' protection. Are they loyal, or not? Can they be counted on in a crisis? Would numbers of them be inclined to shield saboteurs?

The intelligence bureaus were at work long before the war started, finding out the answers to these questions. The Army's G2, the Navy Intelligence, and the FBI, made almost simultaneous public announcements. These were statements that the great majority of Japanese were loyal to the United States and should be treated as friends. The new technique in espionage was in operation.

Shunzo felt certain that the intelligence bureaus were not motivated by a feeling of altruism or YMCA good fellowship when they made this pronouncement, nor were they simply up to tricks. They had become aware of a social situation, and were acting upon the knowledge they had gained. "Until they spoke out," he said, "the Japanese in Hawaii were a sad lot, the second generation in particular. We considered ourselves as American as anyone else, yet we met suspicion every time we tried to act. No Japanese could work at Pearl Harbor. We understood the reason, but we still felt the sting of discrimination. Few Japanese were ever admitted to the National Guard. Of those who were let in, none ever reached higher rank than that of sergeant. The rumor spread that Japanese would not be taken into the Army.

We really were relieved to find ourselves drafted. At least, induction showed that the Army was not suspicious of our loyalty.

"During this period of distrust and suspicion, the local Japanese had become the victims of petty rackets," Shunzo continued. "Salesmen of I AM AN AMERICAN and other patriotic slogans went from house to house in the Japanese communities. If the Japanese woman of the house resisted the sales' talk, the canvasser threatened her with, 'What will your *haole* [white] friends think when they hear that you refused to have an American emblem in your home?' President Roosevelt's picture hangs in virtually every *saimin* stand in the Territory.

"More serious victimization occurred. There was one case which savors of a dime novel. A well-to-do Japanese merchant named Abe was visited in his home one evening recently by a Japanese man who introduced himself and said he was going to the old country soon. Perhaps Mr. Abe would like him to take greetings to friends and relatives? Yes, said Abe, he would. The visitor then asked the merchant to write his name and that of his prefecture in Japan on a piece of paper.

"A few days later the visitor returned. Above Abe's signature was a statement to the effect that if Japan and the United States should go to war, the undersigned would be loyal to Japan and would assist Japanese spies in Hawaii.

"Letting Abe stew in fright for a while, the racketeer

went to another merchant named Kosuma and played the same trick on him. Then into the picture came an accomplice, a Japanese man named Tokunaga. He called on the two victims, to whom he represented himself as a United States Military Intelligence officer. He told them that he had power to arrest and court-martial them. He was a kind man, however, he said, and would let them go for a consideration of one thousand dollars each. The frightened Japanese paid up. The Naval Intelligence and the FBI learned of the matter and the impostors were arrested."

Then it was, Shunzo said, that the authorities addressed the Japanese community publicly, telling them that they had nothing to fear, that they should not permit themselves to be victimized, and that they were needed by the United States Government to aid in the defense program.

The Japanese of all classes enjoyed a great sigh of relief. They rushed to express their intense gratitude. They saw in these officials *haole* champions whom they had long needed. "We second-generation Japanese formed a committee. What could we do to show our loyalty and to become a part of the defense program?

"First," Shunzo said, "our committee drafted a petition to Secretary of State Hull, asking him to negotiate with the Japanese Government in order to simplify the procedure of expatriation. Then we went out to get signatures. In three weeks, 30,000 Japanese of sixteen years of age or over had signed the petition. It is now in Mr. Hull's hands."

The Japanese had done what they could for the time being to demonstrate their loyalty. Now the committee came back to the intelligence bureaus to find out how to co-operate in the defense program. After a second talk, they formed the Oahu Citizens' Home Defense Committee. Membership in this organization is open to all races, but most of the present members are Japanese.

The Committee was just getting under way when Japan attacked. Its first official action was in response to the call for blood donors. Overnight they signed up more donors than had been obtained from all other racial groups in Honolulu combined. They have now pledged themselves to get two thousand.

Sixty key men from this group, of whom Shunzo is one, are co-operating with the intelligence bureau of the Honolulu police, which has been trained by the FBI. These men are residents of different Japanese communities throughout the islands. Their names are known. They are not engaged in espionage work, but receive reports from any members of their districts who have reason to suspect sabotage. Many of the suspects who have been escorted in since Sunday were turned in by the Japanese community itself. Thus by tapping the resources of Japanese loyalty, the three intelligence bureaus have done a thorough job of sleuthing as well. "Their method, however, is a democratic one," Mr.

Sakamaki said, somewhat in his role of political science professor. "The organization is not spending its time, Gestapo-like, spying on the public. It is answering the public's demand to investigate possible enemies of its safety. The great majority of us Japanese here believe in democracy, and we are determined to root out the few in our midst who are not loyal to America. This is *not* Japan."

At no time since the war talk started years ago have we islanders thought that the Japanese in Hawaii would turn into a mass of saboteurs. We applauded when an Army spokesman a couple of years ago said that any idea of isolating the Japanese population by removing them all to one island had been abandoned. We have lived with them long enough to feel that they have the same ambitions, desires, and weaknesses that we have.

The local Japanese did not fail us. Police Chief Gabrielson told me, "There has not been one single act of sabotage committed by a Japanese." Quite the contrary. They jumped in where all Americans jumped—into the line of blood donors, to the wheels of ambulances, to surgery as doctors, nurses, attendants. Many a soldier seriously wounded at Hickam Field owes his life to the swift work of keen Japanese volunteer surgeons.

At Hickam Field two Japanese boys at work on a defense project when the attack began saw a machine gunner having trouble setting up his gun. They ran to help. After aiding him to anchor it, they fed the ammunition to him while he fired. They loaded so fast that both of them had to be given emergency treatment for burns. When a Nipponese plane fell near them, they ran out and clipped the insignia off the pilot's shoulders for souvenirs.

There is a good story of a local Japanese boy who was said to have been on guard duty on the other side of the island when a Japanese officer from a damaged submarine climbed out and waded ashore. The local boy challenged the officer, first in English, then in Japanese, but got no reply either time. Then he walked up to the officer and slapped him.

"Do not strike me," the officer said, in perfect English. "I am a gentleman and expect to be treated as such."

"Gentleman, hell!" the local Japanese boy said, "you're one of those bastards that's responsible for me being out here on guard duty at twenty-one dollars a month!" And, smack! he slapped the officer again.

The findings of the FBI, and of the Army and Navy Intelligence services have borne us out in our estimate of the loyalty of the Japanese in Hawaii. Of all the people on Oahu, only 273—and by no means all of them Japanese—have been detained as suspicious characters.

When Japanese aliens have been falsely suspected, they have taken the experience of detainment with philosophic understanding. One of these detainees who was subsequently released wrote the following charming letter to the commander of the camp:

> I am very sure that all those detainees are fairly treated and all are satisfying at the camp. They are also willing to cooperate with you and warden and they are wishing to set example of good detainees so you can depend on them as much as cooperations are concern.
>
> All are enjoying three good meals a day, but lack of vegetables and fruit and if it is permissible I do not mind to send papaias and bananas not every day but occasionally. I live in a country where many farmers and they are too glad to serve with their own products.
>
> If I am allow to suggest a few things which I thought were good. Detainees want to read some things to keep up their moral and an English Gospel's such as St. John, St. Luke, St. Mark and St. Matthew will enlighten them very much and also if checkers, cards or indoor ball material for recreation will cheer them up very much and if it's permissionable, I am sure churches and Y.M.C.A. are too glad to send them in. . . .
>
> In closing I wish to repeat thanks for your very good treatment while I was in the detention camp. Thank you again and again.

The authorities at the detention camp followed his suggestions. No, this is not Japan.

Everyone in Hawaii, Japanese as well as the rest of us, felt relieved and gratified when it was officially announced that not a single act of sabotage had been committed since the war began. The "new methods" initiated two years ago by democrat Shivers seemed to be working. The authorities are taking no chances, but neither are they terrorizing the populations.

"How long do you think your method would last in Japan?" someone asked Mr. Shivers.

"This is not Japan," he replied.

# The Niihau Story

EVERYONE IN HAWAII was thrilled and delighted with "the Niihau story," as it was immediately called. We were delighted because the irrepressible Hawaiians had not failed us. No matter how history has passed them by, when it comes down to the fundamentals of manhood and womanhood—the good old eternal virtues of courage and loyalty—the Hawaiians are right there, fighting with the rest. It pleased us, too, because it localized the war, made it Hawaii's war, to a degree at least. Dog-fights have taken place above battle-fields the world over, but "the Niihau story," with all its circumstances of locality and Hawaiian character, could never have occurred anywhere else.

Whatever happens on Niihau is of exceeding interest to us in Honolulu simply because nothing ever happens on this little isle 120 miles away—or if it does we do not hear about it because we have no means whatever of communicating with it. This story began soon after the attack on December 7. Honolulu papers did not get it until December 16. That's how it is on Niihau. No telephones, no radios—either sending or receiving—no wireless, or two-way communication of any sort even with her neighbor Kauai, only thirty miles away. The little community of fewer than two hundred Hawaiians on Niihau have led their own peaceful lives away from the rest of the world. Yet when America went to war, this most remote and peace-loving of all her communities was brought into the battle on the very first day.

It was about one o'clock when a single-seater plane flew low over the little island and zoomed to the ground in a crash.

Hawila Kaleo-hano ran out of his house and saw the cracked-up plane with the emblem of the Rising Sun on its wings. A Japanese pilot was lying in the dirt a few feet away. While the flyer was still dazed, Hawila took his pistol and some papers. Hawila had not heard of the war.

Hawaiian men, women, and children came running from their small homes.

"What shall we do?" they asked each other. Nothing of the kind had happened on Niihau since any of them could remember. Nor had their parents ever included such a strange thing in all their stories of fish and gods.

"Treat him with *aloha,*" they said. "The poor man is hurt. Let us take him to Mr. Robinson's house."

Mr. Elmer Robinson, of Kauai, is the owner of the island. His is the largest house on Niihau. When in the past any guest had arrived—though guests were rare—they had gone to Mr. Robinson's.

So by means of two Japanese who had lived on Niihau for many years, they informed the flyer of their intentions, and then accorded him the most hospitable treatment with which Niihau could favor any visitor.

After resting for two days and nights, eating well from the bounty of his Hawaiian hosts, the enemy pilot began to scheme. He learned from Harada, one of the Japanese, with whom the pilot had become friendly, about the motor-sampan that came over from Kauai every Friday with mail and goods. When it returned to Kauai this Friday, it would carry his story. It would come back to Niihau with soldiers.

Perhaps the pilot thought, "Why not turn my stumbling block into a stepping stone? I can use a motor-sampan. Maybe I can reach the Carolines in it."

He had a long talk with the two Niihau Japanese. He was persuasive. Possibly he spoke in nostalgic terms of Japan, of one's duty to the Emperor, no matter how far one may be from snow-capped Fujiyama and the green isles of home. Perhaps he threatened to kill them if they did not do as he said.

Harada went out on a search for the pistol which Hawila had taken from the pilot and hidden.

Shintani, the second of the Niihau Japanese, knocked at Hawila's door. Could he have the papers that Hawila had in keeping for the pilot? The flyer was well now and would like to have them back.

"No," said Hawila.

The pilot was willing to pay.

*"Huakele!"* ("Get out—fast!")

Shintani became frightened. What would the pilot do to him if he returned without the papers? He ran off into the woods and hid there.

An hour later Hawila looked out of his window and saw Harada, the pilot, and a Hawaiian youth approaching his house. Looking closely, the man in the house saw that Harada had the pistol in the youth's back. Hawila slipped out the back way. The pilot searched the house, but did not find the "war papers."

Hawila ran to warn the village.

The two Japanese were already lifting the machine gun out of the plane. The Japanese pilot turned on the radio, but it would not work. They set the machine gun up in a carriage belonging to the Robinsons, trained it on the village, and started firing. The terrorized people fled out their back doors to the woods and seashore caves. This was on Friday. After nightfall, when the two Japanese made a great bonfire of Hawila's house and the wrecked plane, Hawila persuaded five other Hawaiians to make a break with him. They ran to the barn for their horses, leaped on them bareback, and dashed away under the fire of the pilot's machine gun.

They rode eighteen miles to the beach at Kii, where an emergency whaleboat lay. Pushing off in it, the men rowed steadily for ten hours to cross the rough thirty-mile channel. They landed on Kauai early Saturday morning.

Army authorities dispatched a local Japanese, Lieutenant Mizuha, and a squad of men from the 299th Infantry to return to Niihau and round up the enemy.

Meanwhile, developments on Niihau were not waiting for the rescue party. While the party was debarking from Kauai, on Niihau the pilot and his man Harada set out to find Hawila, intending to force him to surrender the papers (probably maps). They searched in the caves along the seashore. Hawila was not there. They captured a Hawaiian named Benjamin Kanahele and his wife in one of the caves and forced him to help in the search for Hawila.

Benjamin knew that Hawila had escaped to Kauai, but pretended to search. His wife followed her husband.

"Hawila! Hawila!" Benjamin Kanahele's voice echoed through the woods. He led the party to a wall made of jagged lava rock.

The pilot realized that this was a wild-goose chase. His brown face turned red. Sweat stood out on his forehead. He yelled in rage to Harada.

"He is going to shoot you and everyone on the island if you do not find Hawila," Harada told the Hawaiian couple. The pilot carried a shotgun he had taken from one of the houses—the only firearm in Niihau's arsenal. His pistol stuck out of one of his boots.

Harada was carrying the cartridges. At a sign from the pilot, Harada handed him the cartridges, taking the shotgun. At the moment the shotgun passed hands, the six-foot Hawaiian jumped the Japanese flyer.

The Japanese jerked his pistol from his boot and tried to shoot, but Kanahele's wife, following the example of Hawaiian women of old who went to battle with their men, rushed in and grabbed his arm.

The flyer yelled at Harada in Japanese. Harada struggled with the strong Hawaiian woman. She had to let go the pilot's arm. He shot Kanahele. The bullet went into his ribs. The wounded Hawaiian jumped the Japanese again. The pilot shot him again, this time in the hip. He shot a third time and hit the Hawaiian in the groin.

"Then," Kanahele said to the English interpreter to whom he later told the story, "I got mad."

The enraged Hawaiian came down upon the Japanese like a killer whale upon a shark. He seized him bodily and hurled him with a terrific slam against the lava stone wall.

Then he remembered that Harada had the shotgun. He turned and saw Harada clumsily placing the muzzle of the gun to his stomach, trying to shoot himself. He was in such a hurry that he missed as the shotgun kicked itself out of his hands. He grabbed it up, placed it against his stomach again. This time he succeeded, and the gun did its work.

Kanahele wheeled to see if the pilot was getting to his feet. He was not. The Hawaiian's wife was rushing in again to her husband's aid. She grabbed a big rock.

"She was plenty *hu-hu* [angry], that woman," Kanahele said. "She started right in to beat that pilot's brains out. She did a pretty good job."

By this time, Benjamin Kanahele, with three bullets inside him, was not feeling well. He sat down by the stone wall. His wife ran to the village for help. But while aid was coming on horseback, he grew tired of waiting, got up and walked to the village alone.

In Hawaii we said, "This is the story of Niihau, an epic of tragedy and heroism. This is the story of true Hawaiian warriors, Benjamin Kanahele and his loyal wife."

And we said, "Warn the Japanese not to shoot Hawaiians more than twice. They get mad the third time."

# *Two Months After*

AFTER THE FIRST week of the war, I thought that if you were to visit Hawaii for the first time, or even return after a long absence, you would not at once find it remarkably different from what you expected. More things are unchanged than changed. The contour of the island has not changed. The glorious heights are still here, and the deep valleys. All the landmarks you look for from the ship—Diamond Head, the clouds above Tantalus, the light showers turning the upper valleys purple, the welcoming green foliage—all these, even down to Aloha Tower and the big pineapple-shaped water tank high above the cannery, are the same.

I have not used the gasoline necessary to take me to see the view from the pali since the war started, but they say it is even more wonderful when you walk, as I intend to do soon. We do not move about at night now, but sometimes in the evening I walk on the back lawn. It is very quiet now that so few cars pass, and the moonlight seems even more brilliant than ever, lighting up the blossoming mango trees and falling clear on wide spaces of lawn.

We old-timers claim that Waikiki, the tourist haven, has improved. It is not crowded. Usually I swim from Gray's out to the raft a couple of hundred yards away, then down to Fort DeRussy. The other day, as I swam to within ten or fifteen strokes of the raft, I saw a fence of barbed wire stretching from the raft toward one part of the shore, keeping the Fort free and the channel clear of visitors. Fortunately you cannot see the barbed wire from Waikiki—but you are glad to know that the Army is taking no chances.

If you know Honolulu well, you will soon discover the changes. One of the most striking is that of Punahou School, long famed as "the oldest school west of the Rockies." Its boast is that in the rough Forties and Fifties of the past century residents of Oregon and California used to send their children to Punahou rather than allow them to brave the trip across country to the East. Punahou celebrated its double-golden anniversary just last June. Before it was well started on its hundred and first year, the war struck.

The very first night, according to well-formed plans, the U.S. Engineers moved into the spacious grounds, took over the buildings, and began working fast. Several of the girls and teachers living in the dormitory woke up Monday morning to find themselves reclining in an army canteen. A few teachers stayed on, ladling out soup to hungry workers.

The detail of the campus which has weathered the

change best is the stone wall, made of lava-rock and covered with a vigorous hedge of night-blooming cereus. The jagged rock and the prickly cactus plant match the mood of bayonets and barbed wire very well. Townspeople have always come out at night in droves when the hundred-year-old cereus hedge blossoms. It is probably the most gorgeous of its kind in the world, stretching for over a mile, and throwing thousands of golden centered white lanterns open to the moon. When it blossoms again, it will be for the eyes of the U.S. Engineers alone. Nobody travels at night, and by day the flowers are wilted. . . . And the Engineers will not have time to look at them!

The broad green campus of the University of Hawaii is zig-zagged with trenches. If the University opens for the second semester, professors and girls—there will be few, if any, boys—will leap into them when shrapnel starts flying.

University people, like everyone else in Honolulu, have been working full-time and overtime since December 7. Experts in languages were already in touch with the Navy Intelligence. They had snatched Dr. Denzel Carr, who speaks thirty languages and reads over fifty, long before the war started.

Japanese professors are helping the FBI. Biologists and chemists are continuously taking samples of water from different parts of town, testing them for poison or harmful bacteria. Dr. Allen says people hear that tests are being made and immediately find something wrong with their water. "It tastes funny," they claim, until it is proved pure. Dr. Allen is quite reassuring. He says the Japanese would have to pour a ship-load of arsenic into our water supply before they could poison the population.

Scores of faculty members and staff are engaged in the tremendous project of taking a careful census and then fingerprinting everyone in the Territory. The entire Department of Agriculture was moved at once into the division of food supply in the Civilian Defense office.

Our "friends" of the business world are saying that one good thing the war has done is to put us university professors to work!

Of course, you would miss regular mail. Now that we have convoys, we never know when mail is coming or going, and occasionally there are long lapses. If you are eager to hear from people you love, you may be unnecessarily upset. Fortunately, you can still send a wire and even telephone. Censors are everywhere, but they are interested in suppressing only information that might be helpful to the enemy.

I talked to my wife in New York a few nights ago, and it was the best thirteen dollars I ever spent. I had been warned not to mention any names of persons, places, or ships, the weather, any movement of troops or numbers of planes. I had no such information. Even so I broke the rules three or four times before I knew it—the first thing I said was "Ruby!" It was a name, and so tabu, but it is hard to talk to your wife without mentioning her name.

The story is told of a newly wed army wife whose husband was on emergency duty and did not get home for a week. She rang him up every day. The fifth day she said, "I don't care if that old thing is listening in, I'm going to tell you I still love you!"

Mr. Frear read in the paper one morning an Army order to the effect that every man on the island would be expected to procure his own tools and build an air-raid shelter, large enough to protect himself and the members of his family. We immediately got to work. I suggested the location—that is, I said I thought it ought to be in the back yard rather than the front. Mr. and Mrs. Frear selected the exact location under a kiawe tree near the sundial where Ruby and I were married. They furnished the tools. All Yamato had to do was throw out the dirt. It is a trench, seven feet deep, two and a half or three feet wide, and forty feet long, and we are very proud of it.

It has a zig, a zag, and a zig. We enter at either zig and stand in the covered zag. The theory is that if shrapnel enters either zig it will fly into the dirt wall and not reach us. Yamato has planted tomatoes in the pile of fresh dirt around the shelter and on top of the zag.

The shelter was first used a few days ago. A long alarm was sounded from Aloha Tower and from other warning signals recently installed in the various sections of town. Some of the Punahou girls who were having classes here at the house, ran gleefully into it. Unfortunately I could not join them. I was in a bus on the way to Kaneohe, and the busman did not stop. A series of short blasts told us it was over. It was announced later that somebody got the signals crossed and sounded the long alarm for the beginning, when it should have been the short. From now on, short blasts will announce the alarm; a long one, end it.

Last month you could get ten gallons of gasoline, no matter who you were. If you could show cause, you could get more. I ran out in two weeks. A student who was in my Eighteenth Century class the first semester gave me a five-gallon ticket and saved me. I have a strong presentiment that if we open the University again the second semester, she will get an A! This month you have to be a useful person in order to get any gas at all—a worker in an institution, a business house, or on a defense project. I am a member of an institution at present defunct, and am just wondering what the tough U.S. Engineers will say when I try to describe the writing of a book as a defense project.

If you have friends in Hawaii and want to send them something they will like, send a map and a flashlight with some extra batteries. All the maps in town were sold out the day after the war started. Some of us here hardly know where the fighting is. We hear Kuala Lumpur mentioned on the radio, and it sounds bad for the British, but that's about all.

The flashlight, of course, is for use while we wander about in the parts of the house not blacked out. I have been surprised to learn how badly I can get turned around in a house where I have lived for months at a time. I always thought there were fourteen steps leading up to my bedroom, but the first night I stumbled on the fifteenth and then again on the sixteenth. Try putting toothpaste on your toothbrush in the dark. I usually get too much. And taking a bath! A fellow at Kaneohe said he had great difficulty because he lost his soap in the bathtub, but that he was getting along all right now since he had bought some black soap. Sol Pluvius, local weather man and humorist, said that if any one with a black eye claimed he got it by running into a door, he was probably telling the truth.

It takes about twice as long to make up a bed in the dark as in daytime. I have found that the easiest way is to get in the bed first. Pull the sheet up and smooth it out to each side of the bed. Then the first blanket, then the second. If the sheet needs to be tucked in at the bottom, turn on the— "For God's sake, put out that light before the policeman shoots it out!"

Some unlucky persons have not yet blacked out any room in the house, so that they have to eat early and then sit around in complete darkness. Even so, they are not much worse off than those who have not figured out some kind of scheme for ventilating the room that is blacked out. One way to do it is to make a zig-zag entrance and leave the door open.

I feel guilty whenever I tell anybody here about our luxurious blackout room. It's air conditioned. The three of us sit here in perfect comfort, turning the conditioner up or down as we wish to change the temperature of the room. I sit here at the typewriter, Mrs. Frear knits for the Red Cross, reading from a book on a stand set up in front of her, and Mr. Frear works busily revising his account of Hawaii in the *Encyclopædia Britannica* so that the new edition will include the attack on Pearl Harbor.

We all knock off for the news. At seven o'clock Mr. Frear bends over close to the radio and listens to every word Jim Wahl says on the Shell News program, again for Bill Norwood at 7:30, and once more for the CBS round-the-world news. If a man's voice continues on the radio directly after the news is over, Mr. Frear listens intently to catch any late bulletin. Frequently he bends his ear close and hears "Buy the tonic that will give you hair that men, and especially women, admire." He raises his heavy gray eyebrows, smiles, and shakes his head as if to say, "I don't need any of that!"

Just like you in San Francisco and New York and

London, we have a wag who has turned his attention to air-raid instructions. For those interested in comparative literature, I reproduce our "regional" creation:

1. As soon as bombs start dropping, run like hell. It doesn't matter where, as long as you run! Wear track shoes, if possible. If the people running ahead of you are slow or fall down, you won't have any trouble passing them or running over them.
2. Take advantage of opportunities afforded you when the air-raid sirens sound the warning of attack or blackout. For example:
   A. If in a bakery, grab a pie.
   B. If in a tavern, grab a beer.
   C. If in a theater, grab a blonde.
3. If you find an unexploded bomb, pick it up and shake it; maybe the firing pin has stuck.
4. If an incendiary bomb is found burning in a building, throw gasoline on it—you can't put it out anyway, so you might just as well have a little fun.
5. When the first bombs fall, holler bloody murder. It will add to the fun and confusion, and scare hell out of the kids.
6. It's well to have onions and limburger handy as a snack before entering a crowded air-raid shelter. It may make you very unpopular, but you'll have lots of room for yourself.
7. If you should be the victim of a direct hit, don't go to pieces. Just lie still and the sanitation squad will take care of you.
8. If an air-raid warden starts to tell you what to do, knock

him down. Wardens always save the best seats for themselves and their friends.

People in Hawaii would feel ashamed if I made you think that we take the war lightly. We joke about the blackout and the gasoline restrictions, but we are also proud of General Emmons' statement that our blackout is more successful than London's. If we laugh, it is because we know that compared to the sacrifices made by our soldiers and sailors, our little civilian sacrifices are trivial.

Honolulu morale is high. We have learned that our civilian morale is the result of our preparedness. We see that morale depends upon what goes on before the war hits. The Hawaii Medical Association is treasuring a telegram from George Baehr, M.D., Chief Medical Officer for Civilian Defense in Washington. It reads:

> Territorial Medical Association: Office of Civilian Defense requests you urge all hospitals to establish immediately emergency medical field units in accord with plan outlined in Medical division bulletin Nos. 1 and 2 and drill weekly. When necessary, reserve field unit should be organized with Medical G. W. nursing and training volunteer personnel derived from the community. Urge immediate action.

This telegram arrived just two and one-half days after twenty such units had been in action. To appreciate the preparation it takes to train a complete medical unit, you must know that a single unit consists of two doctors, two dentists, eight nurses, eight surgical aides, eight supply men, one supply clerk, six stenographers, nine utility men, sixty-four litter bearers, two dietitians, two motorcyclists, two messengers, six ambulance drivers, and three ambulances. One hundred and twenty persons in all. When you remember that the Hawaii Medical Association had twenty units, a total of 2400 persons, in the field on the morning of the bombing, you see what a deal of preparation the doctors had made.

Each one of the 2400 persons who sprang to activity on that December Sunday had received eighty-two hours of instruction. For months busy doctors voluntarily met groups of people in hot schoolrooms after work at night. It was boresome, tiring labor. They had "dry-runs," rehearsing an emergency, pushing ambulances out, carrying each other around on stretchers, and wrapping each other up in bandages. All this shadow-play seemed foolish to people looking on from the outside who did not think there was going to be any emergency anyway.

But on Sunday, their preparation gave spirit to the rest of us and, in many cases, an outlet to our own energies. The marvelous expression of public desire to help by contributing blood could not have happened had Dr. Pinkerton and others not already had the blood bank in working order. Doctors who worked at Pearl Harbor do not like to think what those first six hours would have been like without the plasma that was already in the bank and that was rushed to them by Dr. Pinkerton. They are mighty glad that the far-sighted Doctor pushed the idea of a blood bank months ago. Some persons had thought he was a scare-monger.

"A thousand flasks of blood plasma! What did the man think was going to happen? A war?" The Doctor did not get his thousand, but the 210 he did get proved to be such a godsend that they inspired the whole community.

# *Remember Pearl Harbor!*

I HAVE HAD my wish. I have lived history. The audacious attack on Pearl Harbor is of world-wide significance. For one thing, it gives us in Hawaii and, I should think, everyone on the mainland United States a new conception of the strength of the Axis Powers. We heard many cock-and-bull stories here about Japanese lack of initiative and imagination—that any ability they possessed was solely imitative. If we had believed some, we would have thought that every ship in the Japanese Navy would fall over on its side if it steamed into rough water. Now we have learned the hard way.

No matter how much we despise the Japanese Naval Command which planned and executed one of the most treacherous and despicable stabs in the back ever given any nation, we have to hand it to them. The bold-faced treachery of it surpasses even Hitler's attacks on peaceful nations. But, like Hitler, they delivered the first blow well. If you can forget the ethics of it, you are forced to admit—I will not say to admire—the imaginative daring of the attack. For one hour and twenty minutes, the Japanese air and naval forces achieved the impossible.

We in Hawaii were amazed and flabbergasted when we tried to analyze "how it happened." We refused to dwell on this question. We suppressed vain speculation and awaited the report of the investigating committee. No matter what else that report revealed, it gave implicit testimony to the long-time, skilled planning of the Japanese. Their imperialist and military rulers are desperate but strong.

Japan is not acting alone, but in collaboration with the other members of the Axis. We think she has put her money on the wrong horse. Nevertheless, it is highly significant that she made the Axis her choice to win. We are confident that Japan is wrong, and that Russia and Britain will continue to deal Germany and the Axis crushing blows. But here in Hawaii we have learned that it is important to act as though the thing which we believe cannot happen, may happen. We believe that it is necessary to act as if Russia and Britain may not crush the Axis.

We hear phrases like "Commit national hara-kiri," which suggest that the Japanese have wilfully thrown themselves into this war as a dramatic, desperate, but hopeless gesture to preserve their national honor. Though all of us have the deepest, sincerest respect for the gallant defenders of Wake Island, Hong Kong, Manila, and Kuala Lumpur, the fact is that these places fell. Japan lost heavily there and at Pearl Harbor, but she did not commit hara-kiri. Far from it. Japan is on the offensive. She has not proceeded according to schedule, perhaps, but she has proceeded—and is still proceeding. If she takes Singapore—and the city is in mortal danger at this writing—she has only to consolidate her gains to continue with her far-sighted, daring plan.

We have learned the strength of the Axis, but that knowledge has brought us the blessing of consolidation. Here in Hawaii, as in the whole United States, Pearl Harbor has merged all groups into common action. We had our fascist-minded people, just as the mainland had. We had individuals here who were inclined to do business with Hitler—who did not admire him, perhaps, but who envied him his lack of labor problems. We had our America Firsters. . . . To be sure, they, like their friends in the States, joined in the clamor of indignation that rose against the attackers . . .

Since feeling the muscle of the Axis, we feel much nearer to it. We had a taste of blitzkrieg. The Nazi-Fascist technique hit us. The physical parallels between the attack on us and those on German-occupied countries reminded us directly of other parallels between Japan and the Axis. Before that Sunday, we believed our books and the accounts of our foreign correspondents, but we paid little attention to them. They told us of Japan's suppression of dangerous thoughts, her expulsion of university professors, her re-writing of standard history according to the fascist pattern, and her persecution of foreign students for liberalism. I myself have traveled in Japan and been followed by her agents. Many of us here have; but until Pearl Harbor, we only laughed at the naïveté of the Japanese. We believed, but we forgot.

Now, no matter how we hate and despise the Japanese imperialists, just as we hate those who paid Hitler, we no longer say they are naive, any more than Hitler is naive. Japan's imperialists see clearly what they must do at home and abroad in order to survive. At home, they have probably succeeded. It seems—and we should act as if it were true—that the fascist mind has completely dominated the population. We have even less hope of a revolution in Japan than in Germany.

Japan claims that there were suicide pilots in the attack on Pearl Harbor. Our Navy does not think so. Two "suicide submarines" were caught. It is believed that these small craft were launched some two hundred miles from Pearl Harbor. The Tokyo radio insists proudly that the whole attacking force was an immense mass suicide squadron. We do not have to condescend to believe the Tokyo radio in order to grant that the Japanese rulers have achieved a temporary blind obedience to them and to the Emperor that is exceedingly dangerous to us.

What kind of conditioning would make a suicide submarine operator lie alone in the dark caverns of the sea, waiting an opportunity to die in the muck of the ocean? What produces such fanatic loyalty to the Emperor and to the ruling class which he represents? We cannot help asking ourselves these questions. In the answer to them we seek some explanation of the attack.

Groping for these answers, we come with a fresh mind to the old facts which we had let go in one ear and out the other. We recall the want and poverty of the masses of Japan—poverty created by the wholesale appropriation of the nation's wealth and resources into the greedy hands of the five families: the Mitsuis, the Mitsubishis, and the rest. We remember how children are taught superstitious loyalty to the Big Five's friend, Hirohito. How truth is kept from school children from the time they are three years old. How they were never encouraged, as in our schools, to think for themselves, but trained instead to believe that blind, unquestioning loyalty is the supreme virtue.

If the Big Five of Japan had solved Japan's social problem, given Japan's people food, they would not have had to give them fanaticism and superstition. We knew this before, and some had heard it until they were bored, but on that terrible Sunday morning we realized with a jolt that Japan and the Axis will, if they can, impose this intellectual and social blitzkrieg upon us by a blitzkrieg of arms.

It enrages us to reflect that we have permitted some in our midst to prepare Japan for the blitz with which she struck us. Our women and children were killed by scrap-iron which the vast majority of Americans never wanted to go to Japan in the first place. The terrific irony of it, the coldblooded money policy that dictated it, are too much for the most patient to bear. We think it still smells to high heaven, and we spit when we hear the word *appeaser*. If any are left in the State Department, we in Hawaii want them cleaned out!

Right now, when we say "Remember Pearl Harbor!" we are thinking of preparation and war. We are thinking of immediate defense of our actual lives. We are thinking, too, of what makes life worth living in America and why we are willing to die rather than surrender what we have gained in the past two hundred years. We are so convinced of the rightness of the fundamental conception of democracy that we hardly stop to think of it in concrete terms. But we know that it is on the basis of hundreds of pictures of democracy in action every day of our lives that we act now, intuitively, to defend it.

Each of us has his own picture of what it is he is defending. I think at once of Greenfield, Tennessee, the small town where I spent my formative years. Greenfield had a lot of democracy. There was not a home in the town that I, as a growing boy, did not feel welcome to enter and sit down to a meal. I knew the shape and texture of each housewife's biscuits—how Mrs. Lett's always had brown spots of baking powder in them, how Mrs. Hanaway's were small and white. . . . Mrs. MacReady made her own ketchup, spicy and red.

I never knew what it was to feel that someone was "better" than I. Some were stronger, handsomer, brighter, but no Greenfielder would have understood what is meant by class differences. My father probably never made over 150 dollars a month in his life, yet he was one of the town's leading citizens, and I have always been proud of him. I mowed lawns and knew everyone well. They all praised me when I worked hard, and complained if I failed to pull the weeds.

In school I had a square deal. The first year I played football I was accepted as a man by the older fellows who sat on the curb in front of Brasfield's Drug Store every Sunday. Later, at Vanderbilt University, I ran the campus pool room, yet I belonged to a fraternity, went to the dances, and had perfectly wonderful dates every week. My professors encouraged independent thinking. I sat up nights concocting ways to confound "Eddie" Mims and "Cocky" Sanborn and got A's and B's for being a good fighter. I encountered broadmindedness more often than meanness.

In my profession too, I have had a square deal. We have a small university here in Hawaii—small enough still that every professor knows the president. We do not have a teachers' union, because not enough professors feel that they need it. Whenever some of us decide that we want one enough to work for it, we can have it. In the meantime, we talk things over with the president.

Before I had written a book, I suspected that getting

a manuscript accepted probably depended upon pulling strings, getting a good agent, meeting somebody who would introduce me to somebody. I wrote a book, sent it to two publishers who rejected it for what appeared to be sensible reasons. I sent it to a third, who took it. I wrote another book, which I showed to publishers in New York. Those who rejected it talked about the manuscript in such detail that I felt convinced they had read it and had formed their decision on the basis of the book alone.

My attitude towards the publishers was perhaps naive but my faith in the democracy that exists in America was so renewed that I felt inspired. "If I can write a good book, I can get it published," I thought. That conviction helped me re-write my book. When I finished, the second publisher who saw it took it.

These pictures are in the back of my mind when I hear or read or think "democracy." In the minds of Americans everywhere there are thousands of similar pictures. Each seems trivial, but put together they add up to some mighty impressive facts—the fact of equality of opportunity and the fact of freedom. These are what democracy means to me.

I am no Pollyanna. I know that there are far too many people in the United States who have not experienced freedom and equality of opportunity to the same degree that I have. I remember my own experiences with "big business," first behind a desk in one of Chicago's North Shore hotels and again working for the circulation department of some magazines owned by America's most notorious publisher. Before I had worked in the hotel, no boss had ever tried to make me feel that I was mean, low, of a different class. I hated the manager. When I worked for the publisher, I felt like a prostitute.

If I thought that after this war America was going to be dominated by that type of autocratic mind, I would feel weary and spiritless indeed. I believe that when we have dealt the most powerful autocrats in the world their death blow, we will have an easier time of it with those lesser ones at home. I believe that we will learn—have already learned—from the mistakes of the autocrat-ridden Axis countries. We want not only to preserve our democratic institutions, but to extend democracy—even to the shores of Japan.

The treachery, frightfulness, and ruthlessness of the attack on Pearl Harbor springs from a social system in desperation. A healthy social system does not arm for, nor launch, wars of conquest and acquisition. It does not rear men who will strafe ambulances and civilians in the streets. . . .

When the peace comes, remembering Pearl Harbor will mean remembering the tubercular-ridden, underfed fanatics of Japan, bred by cruelly unjust social relationships. It will mean seeing to it that more equality of opportunity exists in America. It will mean making certain that the people in every country will be allowed to provide for their own livelihood. It will mean permitting these people to set up forms of government that will render fascism and its consequences impossible. Then, not only in war but in peace, will we

***REMEMBER PEARL HARBOR!***